PRINCESS KAIULANI
OF HAWAII

THE MONARCHY'S LAST HOPE

KRISTIN ZAMBUCKA

GREEN GLASS

Published by:
GREEN GLASS PRODUCTIONS INC.
BOX 22525 HONOLULU, HI. U.S.A. 96823-2525

Cover painting by: KRISTIN ZAMBUCKA

Typesetting and book design by:
ARTWORK HOUSE, HONOLULU, HI. U.S.A.

Printing by:
CHINA COLOR PRINTING CO. INC.
TAIPEI, TAIWAN.

ISBN No.: 0-931897-07-7

3RD PRINTING THIS EDITION
JULY 2002

"I must have been born under an unlucky star, as I seem to have my life planned out for me in such a way that I cannot alter it..."

...Princess Kaiulani,
Rozel, Jersey,
summer of 1897.

MANA: *(The Life Force)*
For mana is divine power
And Hawaiians have a keen awareness of this
supernatural force running through all things.
For it is their natural consciousness to be psy-
chic.
And they read signs and omens into elemental
phenomena.
To them, there is nothing that isn't alive.
For everything has mana in some form...
Rocks and plants and mountains, winds and sea.
And water in all its forms is the symbol for this
mystical power called mana...
Water in all its changing moods:
Wailele; the waterfall...
Ua; the rain...
Uhiwai; the mist...
Kahawai; the gentle stream...
And moana; the mighty ocean.

MAKA MUA: *(The beginning)*
For they knew the origin of all life...
And they saw that the universe began in motion
during Po: the cosmic night of creation...
And a movement of the sky (lani) began against
the earth (honua) and the earth heated like a
womb...
And night and day became the cosmic parents of
earth...

y the close of the fourteenth century, the group of islands known as Hawaii, had settled into four kingdoms individually ruled by great families of nobles known as the *alii*.

The four main islands: Oahu, Kauai, Hawaii and Maui had established rulers while ownership of smaller islands in the chain changed hands frequently as prizes of war. As closely as historians can determine, it was in the year 1758 that a chiefly child named Kamehameha was born at Kohala on the big island of Hawaii. Prophecies of greatness surrounded his birth and he emerged as the conqueror in a number of wars on all the islands. Kauai and Niihau were not conquered, but were eventually ceded to Kamehameha without a struggle.

When Captain Cook visited the islands in 1778/79, the ruling chiefs of each island were being referred to as *"kings"* in the European style.

King Kamehameha, victor, proceeded to restore prosperity to his island kingdom which was in a state of ruin after the long period of civil war that united all the islands. Famine and starvation had decimated the population but, by 1798, under King Kamehameha's guidance, the islands were again highly cultivated with *taro*, yams, bananas, coconuts and breadfruit growing in profusion. Industry flourished, and crime and disorder were brought under control.

The king settled on his home island of Hawaii where he made his court for many years at Kailua.

Offspring of the mighty Kamehameha I were numerous and his sons and grandsons continued to reign after him as Kings Kamehameha II, III, IV, and V.

But their heirs were few. The reigns of the last two Kamehamehas, grandsons of Kamehameha the Great, saw marked changes in the Hawaiian Kingdom. The two brothers both favored a British form of government and American Missionary influence diminished in Hawaii in favor of closer ties with England.

King Kamehemeha IV (Alexander Liholiho) was happily married to Emma Rooke, but their union was marred by tragedy.

The birth of their only child, Albert Edward Kauikeaouli Leiopapa a Kamehameha, was greeted with great joy and celebration throughout the islands. Here was a newborn heir to the throne. But the little prince contracted brain fever (known today as spinal meningitis) and died in 1862 at the age of four. His untimely death shattered the king. Affected by chronic asthma and overwhelmed by grief, he too died a year later aged twenty-nine.

His brother Lot succeeded him to the throne as Kamehameha V. This last Kamehameha was thought to resemble his grandfather Kamehameha I and was described as *"one of the last great chiefs of the olden type."* Under his rule, many ancient *hula* and *kahuna* rituals were revived to the horror of local missionaries. Lot reigned for the same term as his late brother; nine years. He never married and died unexpectedly on his forty-third birthday, December 2, 1872, without naming a successor.

After Hawaii had been without a king for several weeks, the Cabinet decided on an election to name a new ruler. The candidates were William Charles Lunalilo and David Kalakaua both of whom had notable genealogies. Lunalilo was unanimously voted in as the new king. He was gentle and fair-minded, occasionally showing a bright intelligence and wit. But his health was weak. King Lunalilo died of tuberculosis aggravated by alcoholism on February 3rd, 1874, one year and twenty-five days after coming to the throne. He benevolently willed his property to found the Lunalilo Home, a trust in perpetuity for aged and infirm Hawaiians.

An election was again vital to Hawaii's future, as there was still no heir to the vacant throne.

Queen Emma, the widow of Kamehameha IV, now contended for the rulership against David Kalakaua, who announced his candidacy the day after Lunalilo's death. After a stormy election in which supporters of both candidates clashed heatedly, Kalakaua won by thirty-nine votes to six.

He took the oath of office on February 13th, 1874, and the colorful Kalakaua Dynasty came into being.

King Kalakaua's long reign of seventeen years brought about a resurgence of Hawaiian culture, which was characterized by the *hula* once again being danced in public, in defiance of the many oppressive laws introduced by the American Missionary element.

Kalakaua, his brother and two sisters all had a natural gift for music. They composed and sang and spent many evenings in keen, musical competition.

To his regret, Kalakaua remained childless throughout his marriage to Queen Kapiolani. His sister, Liliuokalani was also married but bore no children, while his brother, William Pitt Leleiohoku died of rheumatic fever at the age of twenty-three. He was unmarried. On October 16th, 1875, their sister Princess Likelike produced a precious child, Princess

4

Victoria Kaiulani. The only niece of the king was received with great love into the family and with a burst of rejoicing throughout Hawaii.

The *alii* were dying out. The mighty line of chiefs and chiefesses that had ruled for centuries was drawing to an end. Princess Kaiulani was the last hope of the Hawaiian Monarchy, which was being undermined by foreign influences creeping with alarming swiftness into the islands. On the head of this fragile blossom rested the promise of continuity for the Hawaiian throne. The Hawaiian people looked to her for their future.

After a fifty-five day journey from Auckland, New Zealand, the British brig *Sisters* edged towards the old wharf at the foot of Nuuanu Avenue in the town of Honolulu.

On board were Scottish horticulturist Thomas Cleghorn, his wife and sixteen-year-old son Archie. It was June 17th, 1851.

The Cleghorns traveled to New Zealand soon after Archie's birth on November 15th, 1835, in Edinburgh, Scotland. But a stay en route in the port of Honolulu had inspired Thomas Cleghorn to return some day to the Hawaiian Islands

Despite the barrenness of Oahu in those days, Cleghorn determined to work there as a scientific gardener, but instead started a dry goods store on Nuuanu Avenue between King and Hotel Streets.

Two years later, at the age of fifty-four, Thomas Cleghorn died suddenly of a heart attack while walking home from church.

His grieving widow returned to New Zealand to rejoin other family members in Auckland. But the enterprising young Archie Cleghorn stayed on in Honolulu to continue the business that his father had started.

"A.S. Cleghorn and Co." was boldly painted on a newly erected sign and soon the young proprietor became a very successful merchant necessitating his move to a larger location on the corner of Queen and Kaahumanu Streets. Other branches of his firm prospered on Molokai, Maui and the big island of Hawaii.

Archie was well-liked and respected by the townspeople and became active in civic affairs. By this time he had also fathered three daughters, Helen, Rose, and Annie by a handsome Hawaiian woman named Lapeka. He cherished and supported these children and kept them close to him throughout his life.

Then on September 22nd, 1870, in the reign of King Kamehameha V, Archie Cleghorn, aged 35, married Miriam Likelike, a young Hawaiian Chiefess of nineteen. The ceremony was held at Washington Place in downtown Honolulu, the family home of John Owen Dominis, who had married Likelike's sister, Liliuokalani, eight years earlier. Likelike was a descendant of one of Hawaii's ancient chiefly lines. Born on January 13th, 1851, she was the daughter of Kapaakea and Keohokalole, who were descended from the High Chief Kepookalani, first cousin to King Kamehameha I. Likelike, her sister Liliuokalani and her brothers, Kalakaua and Leleiohoku, were known collectively by the Hawaiians as *"Na Lani Eha"*; the

6

"Four Sacred Ones". They were extremely talented musically and composed songs that became a basic part of the Hawaiian musical repertoire. They formed their own respective glee clubs and vied with one another in a merry round of competition.

Leleiohoku died at the age of twenty-three, but Kalakaua and Liliuokalani lived to become reigning monarchs; the last two sovereigns of Hawaii.

Detailed newspaper accounts followed the honeymoon travels of the handsome couple. The Hawaiian Gazette reported:

"Soon after marriage, Mrs. Cleghorn and her husband visited Auckland, Sydney and Melbourne. During their visit, great attention was shown to the Chiefess by the Governors and the officials of the various colonies, and thus, early in life, she was brought into contact with foreign manners and ideas. Her house was, ever after, thrown open to those who visited the islands, and visitors, distinguished and otherwise, have carried her name and the memory of many kindly attentions to every country of Europe and almost every state in the Union..."

After Kalakaua became King, his brother-in-law, Cleghorn, held various government positions of increasing importance. On succeeding her brother to the throne eighteen years later, Liliuokalani appointed Archibald Cleghorn as Governor of Oahu.

Five years after the Cleghorns' marriage, the only child of their union was born on October 16th, 1875, a baby girl.

She was also the only child born to the Kalakaua dynasty and was to become Heir Apparent to the Hawaiian Throne which was occupied at the time of her birth by her uncle, King Kalakaua.

The King, childless himself, was overjoyed at the arrival of his niece. The infant's mother, Likelike was his younger sister and very dear to him. He wanted all of Honolulu to know that she had produced an heir to the throne and ordered his heavy guns to fire an appropriate salute to the royal child. At four o'clock in the afternoon of that October day, all the bells of the city joined in pealing a joyous welcome that lasted for several hours. An heir had been born to the Hawaiian Throne.

One Christmas day, 1875, in St. Andrew's Episcopal Church, Bishop Willis christened the baby: PRINCESS VICTORIA KAIULANI, KALANINUIAHILAPALAPA KAWEKIU I LUNALILO. She was to become known as Kaiulani which meant *"The Royal Sacred One."*

Her sponsors, King Kalakaua, Queen Kapiolani and Princess Ruth, stood beside the flower-bedecked font. Kaiulani squirmed in her cashmere shawl, as her nurse Kahakukaakoi proudly held her.

Later, there was a state reception at the old wooden palace (later demolished to make way for Iolani Palace).

The Royal Hawaiian Band assembled on the lawn to entertain the elegantly attired crowd while the bandmaster Captain Henry Berger proudly played his newly composed work entitled *"The Kaiulani March."*

During Kaiulani's third year, the Cleghorns moved to reside permanently at their Waikiki property, which was four miles from the city.

Long the abode of Oahu chiefs, the property of Ainahau had many historical associations. One such notable event took place on March 20th, 1798, when Captain George Vancouver anchored his ship directly in front of the area. On coming ashore, he walked through the grounds to meet with the high chiefs of the time.

Originally part of a vast estate inherited by Princess Ruth Keelikolani, Kaiulani's godmother, the area was called *Auaukai*. Young Mrs. Cleghorn renamed it *Ainahau* meaning *"cool land",* and reveled in the breezes from Manoa Valley that kept their home constantly ventilated. At *Ainahau*, Archie Cleghorn was able to use to the full his talent for gardening and landscaping. Years later, *Paradise of the Pacific Magazine* carried the following impressive description of the estate:

Certainly the most beautiful private estate in the Hawaiian Islands is Ainahau. The residence faces the blue Pacific and makes a graceful setting in a spacious area of highly cultivated ground. Ten acres of land are, for the most part, covered with tropical trees, shrubs and vines, the varieties of which almost bewildering, form a veritable garden that would interest a scientist. The approach to the grounds and the main entrance bear little significance of the grandeur of the premises immediately surrounding the house. A long avenue bordered by date palms and many plants leads from the gateway to the residence. Directly in front of the porch, compelling the attention of every visitor, is a majestic banyan tree, 30 years old and the parent of all the noted trees of its species in the city. With its great cluster of central trunks, enormous branches and abundant foliage, it is the King of Trees in this park, and unless destroyed by the woodman will long outlive every other form of vegetable growth in the demesne. Mr. Cleghorn cultivates eight kinds of mango trees, some of which bear the chutney mango which is so highly esteemed in India. The teak is an interesting tree that thrives here, and is now bearing seeds which are freely offered to anyone who desires to start a grove of this valuable wood. Two or three of the spice family are represented, the important one being a cinnamon. Several Washingtonia palms are here, towering almost as high as the coconuts. The latter are scattered everywhere, 500 of them having been planted when Princess Kaiulani was born.

A soap tree, indigenous to China, its fruit being used in the manufacture of saponaceous articles, is one of the novelties and an Indian tree bearing red flower like tiger claws is another. Rubber trees thrive like lantana bushes in the open waste. Camphor is also in a healthy state of development. Monterey cypresses and date palms are numerous. Mr. Cleghorn takes pride in the 14 varieties of hibiscus he is cultivating, two varieties of the Hawaiian kamani tree and a sago palm. Importations from India are many kinds of croton.

Kaiulani was given the ten acres of land named *Ainahau* at her christening. It was a gift from her godmother, the High Chiefess Ruth Keelikolani

n the first ballot voting for the throne ever held in Hawaii, Kalakaua lost to King Lunalilo. Lunalilo was in poor health and reigned barely a year before his death again left the throne unoccupied.

Another election was held and this time Kalakaua won against Queen Emma, the widow of King Kamehameha IV.

Nine years and a trip-around-the-world later, Kalakaua decided that he should have a coronation ceremony as was customary with other monarchs he had met on his travels.

It was a day filled with bright sunshine, and the Royal Hawaiian Band started the ceremony with the Hawaiian national anthem, *"Hawaii Ponoi."* The music was composed by Bandmaster Henry Berger, the words written by King Kalakaua. They began:

> *Hawaii Ponoi*
> *Nana I kou moi*
> *Kalani alii*
> *Ke alii.*
>
> *Hawaii's own true sons*
> *Be loyal to your Chief*
> *Your country's liege and lord*
> *The alii.*

Kaiulani was seven and watched the colorful scene excitedly from a window inside Iolani Palace until her mother swooped her up and rushed her to their place in the procession that was forming in the palace hall.

Outside, the King walked towards the pavillion in a white uniform and a white helmet topped with red, white and blue plumes that lifted in the breeze.

He wore the Order of Kamehameha on his chest plus the decorations of many foreign countries. At his side walked Queen Kapiolani in a long, red, velvet gown.

The rest of the procession followed the King and Queen with the Queen's sisters Kekaulike and Poomaikelani first, then Albert Judd, Princess Kaiulani, A.S. Cleghorn, Princess Likelike, John Dominis (Governor of Oahu) and his wife Liliuokalani.

Kaiulani's two cousins, *"Koa"* and *"Kuhio"*, carried the crowns. They were later to be known as the Princes David Kawananakoa and Jonah Kuhio Kalanianaole.

Kaiulani looked closely at the crowns and saw that they were fashioned of small gold taro leaves encrusted with pearls, diamonds, emeralds, rubies and polished black kukui nuts.

In accordance with ancient Hawaiian tradition, no one was ever allowed to stand above the head of a chief nor put his hands over the head of one. Therefore, in a gesture that was badly misinterpreted by those who were ignorant of this ancient *kapu*, the King automatically picked up the crown and placed it on his own head. He then set the smaller crown on the head of Queen Kapiolani, but not without some difficulty, as her black hair had been piled up on top of her head and bejeweled for the occasion. Eight ladies-in-waiting frantically rearranged the Queen's hair-do before His Majesty could set the crown firmly in place.

Kaiulani remarked to her governess that she thought the crown hurt the Queen as she winced when it was jammed on her head.

Heralding the end of the ceremony, guns boomed in the distance from the decks of battleships anchored in Honolulu Harbor.

The choir filled its lungs with air and burst into the tune, *"Cry Out, O Isles with Joy!"*

Hawaii had seen its first coronation.

MANA O'I'O: *(To believe)*
And pantheons of gods were brought into exist-
ence
For the Hawaiians of old had fertile imaginations
And their religion was all art and poetry...
Rich, colorful and intense in its ceremonies.
But the gods were only decoration
Wood and stone images designed to inspire awe...
Just points of focus.
For the Hawaiians knew of the secret inner flame
a light that never went out for them.
It was always the mana; nature's mystic force that
they worshipped.
And the gods evolved from man's concept of this
mana
And the gods became sources of energy.
And the mana flowed two ways.
For the gods could become enormous storehouses
of mana through the absorption of man's be-
lief in them.
But without the faith of man...the gods died.

13

rom the time she was seven, Kaiulani was an excellent rider, and one of the delights of her childhood was her father's gift of a white saddle pony named Fairy. With a mounted groom in attendance, she trotted around the dusty roads of Waikiki visiting friends and sometimes rode all the way into the city.

Miss Barnes, Kaiulani's first governess, taught her to read and write and, trying out her newly acquired art, the little Princess wrote to her doting godmother, Princess Ruth:

Dear Mama Nui,

Thank you for the nice hat you sent me. It fits so nicely. Mama wanted it, but I would not let her have it. Thank you for the corn and watermelons, they do taste so good. Are you well? With much love from your little girl.

Kaiulani

P.S. I want you to give Miss Barnes a native name.

Sounding a little annoyed with her mother she wrote another letter:

Dear Mama Nui,

I want another hat. Mama Likelike has taken the hat you sent me. Are you better now? When are you coming home?

But *"Mama Nui"* didn't come home. She died on the Big Island of Hawaii in the spring of 1883.

The young Princess Kaiulani greatly missed her godmother, who lavished affection on her and kept a constant stream of presents arriving at Ainahau. Towering six feet tall and weighing over 400 lbs., the controversial Ruth Keelikolani, half sister to the last Kamehameha Kings, was fiercely generous and protective towards those she loved and equally formidable towards those she disliked or mistrusted.

With her passing, many of the traditional island ways disappeared, for she was one of the last high chiefesses of old Hawaii.

The island kingdom would not see her like again.

aiulani's governess, Miss Barnes, of whom the family was very fond, died unexpectedly in 1883. Many replacements were tried out, but their stays at Ainahau were short. The arrival of Miss Gertrude Gardinier from New York was to change this pattern.

Princess Likelike approved immediately of the young woman as the new governess for her daughter who was now ten years old. Kaiulani and Miss Gardinier took to one another on sight. The young New Yorker writing to her parents about the little Princess said: *"She is the fragile, spirituelle type, but very vivacious with beautiful large, expressive dark eyes. She proves affectionate; high spirited, at times quite willful, though usually reasonable and very impulsive and generous."*

She wrote of Princess Likelike as *"small, graceful and stylish with pretty dimpled arms and hands. She has an imperious and impulsive nature and is considered quite haughty by some, but she is very genial in her home and is always most thoughtful and considerate of those she likes."*

Miss Gardinier remained at Ainahau as Kaiulani's governess until the day of her wedding to Mr. Albert Heydtmann in May, 1887.

PALUA: *(Dualism)*
And they knew that male and female dualism were
    symbols of positive and negative in the cre-
    ation of the universe...
Heaven and earth united in marriage
And their union produced the race of man
Wakea was the Sky-father
And Papa was the Earth-mother.
Day was a man
And night was a woman
The sun was a man
and the moon was a woman
The north was male
And the south was female
The sea was masculine
And the land was feminine

As 1884 began, Kaiulani's father seemed troubled by political matters. More and more he spoke with his friends of people like Lorrin Thurston, a young City lawyer whose family had been among the first missionaries to arrive in Hawaii from New England in 1820.

Mr. Thurston has given up law to edit the Bulletin...he is on the side of the sugar planters who are opposing the King's party...what is he up to?

Always allowed to stay in the room while her father discussed politics with his friends, the young Prin-

16

cess sensed from their conversation, a threat to her much loved uncle, *"Papa Moi"*, the King.

Around Christmas of 1886, Kaiulani's mother, Princess Likelike, usually full of life and eager to entertain their many visitors, suddenly became very quiet and withdrew completely from everyone around her.

She went to bed and refused any food that was taken to her. As Likelike grew weaker, a dark atmosphere settled over the big house at Ainahau.

Two family doctors were constantly at the Princess' bedside, but neither could diagnose anything physically wrong with her.

Her brother and sister, King Kalakaua and Princess Liliuokalani, came often to visit her and remained in the darkened room with their beloved younger sister for long periods of time.

Archibald Cleghorn sat stricken, watching the life slowly fade from his young wife. Helplessly, he turned to Liliuokalani and whispered hoarsely, *"What's wrong with her? She's only 36!"*

To further upset the family, ugly rumors were flying throughout Honolulu. *"Likelike is being prayed to death by a powerful kahuna,"* the Hawaiian retainers at Ainahau confided to one another. But no one could believe the stories fully as everyone loved Princess Likelike. Who would want to hurt her?

Then came the news that a huge school of *aweoweo,* a small, red, local fish had been seen in mid-January off the big island of Hawaii where Likelike had once been Governor. The massing of these bright red fish close to shore was always considered the harbinger of death for a member of the Kalakaua family.

On the morning of February 2nd, 1887, Kaiulani was called to her mother's bedside. With a strange flash of insight, Likelike, as though to prepare Kaiulani, told her that she could see her future clearly, that she was to live away from Hawaii for a very long time, that she would never marry and that she would never be Queen.

At four o'clock that afternoon, Princess Likelike died.

NA NALU: *(The waves)*
And they marvelled at the symbols of the ocean...
For a wave at its climax beats against the open thighs of golden sand
And foaming in its ecstasy...sinks its life force into the absorbent, female shore.
For it is a glorious re-enactment of procreation.
And from the beginning of life to its end...
The ocean mirrors the passages of existence on earth.
And even death is but a dark wave that carries the body away in its swift current...
Out to calm waters where it is dissolved
So preparation can begin for re-birth in a new form.

n late January, 1889, Robert Louis Stevenson sailed into Honolulu harbor on the yacht, *Casco.* He and his family had journeyed to Hawaii from the South Seas where the Scottish writer was known as *"Tusitala, Teller of Tales."* Stevenson and King Kalakaua soon struck up a boon friendship and, before too long, the King introduced him to his brother-in-law, Archie Cleghorn, a fellow Scot. Thereafter, Stevenson spent a great deal of time at Ainahau in warm camaraderie.

He was entranced with the beautiful young Princess Kaiulani, and they spent many hours talking together beneath the huge banyan tree in front of the house at Ainahau.

She thought his hair was worn too long, longer than she'd seen on any Hawaiian man, and he was thinner than any of them as illness had eaten greedily into his body. But he held her attention as he told her fascinating stories about the world beyond the coral seas around her island, a world into which she was soon to venture.

Just before she left for school in England, R.L. Stevenson wrote this farewell poem in her small red autograph book:

Forth from her land to mine she goes,
The island maid, the island rose,
Light of heart and bright of face,
The daughter of a double race.
Her islands here in Southern sun
Shall mourn their Kaiulani gone.
And I, in her dear banyan's shade,
Look vainly for my little maid.

But our Scots islands far away.
Shall glitter with unwonted day,
And cast for once their tempest by
To smile in Kaiulani's eye.

He added:

Written in April to Kaiulani in the April of
her age and at Waikiki within easy walk of
Kaiulani's Banyan. When she comes to my land
and her father's and the rain beats upon the win-
dow (as I fear it will), let her look at this page; it
will be like a weed gathered and preserved at
home; and she will remember her own Islands,
and the shadow of the mighty tree, and she will
hear the peacocks screaming in the dusk and the
wind blowing in the palms and she will think of
her father sitting there alone.

Robert Louis Stevenson wrote that Kaiulani was:"… *more beautiful than the fairest flower.*"

Kaiulani left for England in May, 1889. She and Stevenson never met again.

Later Stevenson wrote to his friend W. H. Low, *"I wear the colors of the little royal maid. Oh Low, how I love the Polynesians!"*

In preparation for her departure, Kaiulani received the following authorization from her uncle:

I, Kalakaua, King of the Hawaiian Islands
do hereby give my consent and approval for my
niece Her Royal Highness Princess Victoria
Kaiulani, to leave the Hawaiian Kingdom and
proceed to England on or about the month of May
1889, in charge of and under the care and con-
trol of Mrs. Thomas Rain Walker and to be ac-

companied by Miss Annie Cleghorn.

The Princess to travel entirely incognito (crossed out) and be known as Miss Kaiulani. Her return to the Hawaiian Kingdom to be during the year of Our Lord, One Thousand and Eight Hundred and ninety.

Signed,
KALAKAUA REX
Iolani Palace
Honolulu,
March 20th, 1889.

In April 1889, an announcement appeared in the Honolulu Advertiser.

Hon. A. S. Cleghorn, Collector of Customs will accompany his daughter Princess Kaiulani on her foreign journey as far as San Francisco leaving here May 10.

Mrs. T. R. Walker, the wife of the British Vice-Consul, and Annie Cleghorn, the Princess' half-sister, would accompany her for the rest of the trip to England.

Her education in all subjects, required for a future queen, was to begin.

For her last week in Hawaii, the princess and her father made numerous calls around Honolulu visiting friends and relatives to say good-bye. A sleek pair of bay horses drew the Cleghorns' carriage, and a footman stood on a box at the back.

They called on cabinet members, clergyman, consulates and private homes. Kaiulani's ex-governess, Miss Gardinier, now married, had her first baby. The princess visited her, held the infant in her arms and wiped her tears away as she kissed them both goodbye.

The last call on their rounds was made to the King and Queen at Iolani Palace. *"Mama"* and *"Papa Moi"* bade a warm farewell to their niece as did Aunt Liliuokalani at Washington Place. But the most tears shed that day were for Fairy as she hugged the gentle white pony that had brought so much joy to her childhood.

At noon on Friday, May 10, the S. S. *Umatilla* sailed for California with the thirteen year old Princess on board. Kaiulani, trying to hold back her tears, clung to the wooden railing in front of her. As the ship edged away from the wharf. a huge multi-colored crowd stood waving hands and handkerchiefs and calling out blessings and farewells.

Faces, loved and familiar, began to blur as the ship headed out to sea. The band from a distance sounded metallic and brassy as it played the last strains of the National Anthem, *Hawaii Ponoi*. A knot of people, miniaturized with distance, clustered on the wharf as the watery gulf grew wider.

Kaiulani looked beyond the shore to the majestic blue-green mountains behind Honolulu that stood proudly with clouds like capes, around their shoulders.

With stinging eyes, she tore herself away from the scene and hurried to her cabin. Annie Cleghorn and Mrs. Walker hastened to comfort her, but saw that it would be best to leave her alone with her thoughts.

After a rough, week-long crossing to San Francisco, Cleghorn left his daughter there and returned to Honolulu, After his departure, Kaiulani's tears didn't dry until the train ride across the States brought her to the sprawling, bustling city of New York. Its size was beyond her imagination.

From New York, Kaiulani sailed to Liverpool with her companions, (Mrs. Walker had her two small children with her also.) They disembarked and took the train to Manchester, the smoky midland city, where they spent their first night in England. It was a long way from the soft, balmy air of the Hawaiian Isles.

On June 18, they finally reached the city of London. From there, Kaiulani penned excited letters to her uncle and aunt; the king and queen, describing her visits to the theaters of the West End; art galleries where she was awestruck by the huge canvases of Titian, Rubens and Reynolds; the Crystal Palace and the Tower of London, that bleak stone structure where ravens seemed ever watchful of its visitors. She thought of the young English princes imprisoned within cold stone walls so long ago and Sir Walter Raleigh writing the *History of the World* in that dark cramped room that seemed to her "*like a cave*".

"*I am going to school in the middle of September,*" she wrote to friends back home. "*The name of the school is Great Harrowden Hall in Northamptonshire.*"

It was here at Harrowden Hall in Northamptonshire, England, that Kaiulani attended schoolroom classes for the first time. She had previously been tutored by governesses.

Harrowden Hall, built in the fifteenth century for the Barons Vaux, is located two miles outside the village of Wellingborough and sixty-eight miles north of London.

It became a private school for young ladies in the

1890s under the guidance of Mrs. Sharp, the headmistress.

In October of 1889, while at school at Harrowden Hall, Kaiulani received a mysterious letter from her uncle, King Kalakaua. Much of its meaning was a riddle to her, as he began by questioning her about her life at school, then proceeded to warn her to "*be on guard against certain enemies I do not feel free to name in writing.*" Who was it? Whom did he fear?

Fifteen year old Kaiulani wrote back to him at once, expressing her bewilderment. "*I am quite at a loss to know to whom you refer as not to be relied upon - I wish you could speak more plainly, as I cannot be on my guard unless I know to whom you allude.*" She continued with a mention of the kindness of her guardian Mr. Davies, saying between the lines, "*surely you don't refer to him!*"

She anxiously awaited her uncle's reply, but no explanation ever came.

The King who was beginning to worry those around him because of the illness now showing in his face, left for San Francisco in November, hoping the change would do him some good. He named his sister, Liliuokalani, Regent in his absence.

Two months later, Kalakaua died in San Francisco.

Many years later, after much disillusionment at the hands of "*trusted people*", Kaiulani realized the significance of her uncle's warning.

AKUA: *(God)*
For Kane was the Father in Heaven in pre-Christian Hawaii and within his sacred name, many profound symbols were contained.

*Kanenuiakea... Kane, of the magnificent cross of
    light.*
He was the very source of mana.
*And from him flowed the Waters of Kane; The Wai
    Ola; legendary Water of Life.*
He was everywhere ... pervading all space.
And his power gave life to all living things.

In a feature story, the San Francisco Chronicle in
Dec., 1889, reported: *"King Kalakaua is working on
a theological book that will startle the world..."*

But the book was never published.

Kalakaua became very ill in San Francisco. Doctors diagnosed nephritis, an enlarged heart and cirrhosis of the liver. He was put to bed in his suite at the
Palace Hotel.

Against doctors' orders, the King insisted on attending a Masonic Order ceremonial evening.
Kalakaua was a 33rd degree Mason. On this occasion
he was to introduce; *"The Mystic Shrine"*. Soon after,
his condition worsened and by Monday January 19th
1891, he was in a coma.

With his Hawaiian entourage and other friends
and officials at his bedside, King Kalakaua breathed
his last on January 20th.

Communion services of the Protestant Episcopal
Church were conducted in the King's suite. Rev. J.
Sanders Reed recited passages from the scriptures and
Rev. Mr. Church led the singing of hymns.

The Hawaiians said their own prayers, silently,
with tears.

There was a solemn procession down Market St.
towards the U. S. man-o-war that would carry the

King's body back home.

Fifty feet behind the slow, plumed hearse, veiled in black crepe from head to foot, marched the dead monarch's favorite hula dancer... alone.

> LUAKINI: *(Church)*
> *And never forgetting the One Great God above*
>   *all...*
> *An ancient kahuna prayer; the song of a temple*
>   *priest asks that;*
> *Prayers be projected with force to the Highest God*
>   *of Power...*
> *In the song of the wind from the sun.*
> *Breathe your prayers into God.*
> *So the rain of blessings may fall in response...*
> *For there is only one temple we can truly build.*
> *And it is constructed of intangible materials;*
> *Love, happiness, faith and prayer.*
> *And no outside hands can ever pull it down.*

As the Charleston came into view off Diamond Head, the lighthouse keeper was aghast at what he saw in his telescope; the ship's flags were at half-mast. It could only mean one thing; the King was dead on board.

Diamond Head Charlie ran into town with the terrible news.

Bright welcoming bunting was taken down from buildings and black crepe hung everywhere, even on the palace.

At funeral ceremonies in Honolulu, the golden

feather cloak of Kamehameha the Great lay over King Kalakaua's casket. At the head, Queen Kapiolani sat quietly with her head bowed.

Dan Logan; editor of the Bulletin wrote:

"The torch that burns at midday has been quenched..."

An eye-witness account tells of: *"... The grandest, brightest rainbow ever seen, that formed like a gateway following and leading the King's funeral procession as it made its way to Iolani Palace.*

On the Palace balcony, the bereaved Queen Kapiolani had taken her place with ladies of the court.

At five o'clock in the afternoon, the procession entered the Palace Gates on King St.

The magnificent rainbow was now arched over the mountains behind the Palace.

It maintained its watch until dusk.

"Auwe!" cried the people.

"He alii oia i'o no ka o Kalakaua!" ("Kalakaua is indeed an alii!")

KULANA: *(Station or rank)*
And there is a mana that is charisma...
For a person can be born with a great deal of mana...
an almost visible aura that sets him apart from others.
And some have it gradually fed into them by the faith of their supporters.
When their works and deeds are held high in the minds of those who believe in them.
They are given mana by others...
And it is worn like a great cloak of power.

flaming torch at midday was the symbol chosen for his colorful regime by King Kalakaua. With his death, the torch was doused, but echoes of his turbulent reign still sounded throughout the Hawaiian Islands. He had tried to preserve the old Hawaiian culture, and in so doing, he made many enemies. In his time, there was already a movement underway to get rid of all things Hawaiian.

Constant opposition to his efforts, plus his love for champagne, wore down the King's health. After a seventeen-year reign, he died in January, 1891.

That month brought cold winds blowing from the sea, in Honolulu. The people waited, tense with anticipation, as the King's successor came to the throne - his sister, Liliuokalani. Unlike her dynamic brother, she was reserved and quiet, and she began her reign in mourning; not just for her brother, but seven months later she lost her husband, the frail Governor John Dominis. *"At a time when I needed him most...,"* she wrote in her diary.

The new Queen was burdened with troubles, most of which she thought were inherited, so she promptly dismissed the old cabinet which had served Kalakaua, She considered them incompetent. She then appointed her own Ministers. Subsequently, many cabinets came and went, during Liliuokalani's brief reign.

HUA: *(To bear fruit)*
But a new flowering had already begun...
For the Hawaiians' natural habit of frequent
prayer was never broken...
And they saw that the people of the new faith also
prayed often.

*And with "baptism" they cleansed themselves in
the sea.*

So like their old Hawaiian ritual.

*And their ho'o'pono'pono become "confes-
sion"...*

*And so the Christian God was placed in a Ha-
waiian setting.*

And his altar was new... but it was the same God.

*For a rainbow may fade... but it is still there...
vibrant and colorful in the mind's eye.*

And so it still exists.

A dry leaf drops...

but a new green shoot is already sprouting...

The sun may set here...

But it is already rising somewhere else.

*Dawn is always hidden in the sunset... just as faith
lives on*

"Give love and hospitality and trust..." they said.

For all will be returned to you..."

*And they knew that these were the qualities that
colored this earthly life.*

At the age of fifty-two, Kalakaua's sister
Liliuokalani was proclaimed Queen on Jan.
30th 1891.

She was a devout Christian and attended church
services regularly. Following her accession to the
throne, a special koa pew was installed in Kawaiahao

Church for her use.

Married to John Owen Dominis since 1862, the Queen had no children.

The first year of Liliuokalani's reign saw great rivalry between foreign businessmen and native politicians as they jostled for positions of power in the new administration.

To add to the new queen's concerns, Hawaii was obviously headed for an economic depression, when foreign sugar was allowed into the United States free of duty and Hawaii's sugar was no longer wanted.

During her first few months on the throne, Liliuokalani made plans to place her people *"back on the land."* and give *"Hawaii back to the Hawaiians."* She opened up thousands of acres of Crown Lands on the Big Island and waived all rentals until the people settled in comfortably. The land became occupied quickly.

OLELO: *(The word)*
And they knew the roots of certain words contained keys to unlock the mysteries of man.
And foster him while he rises on the eternal spiral.
For some words are heavily charged with mana.
And when something is said, its existence has begun.
For words are forces in themselves.
Angry words are angry actions
And words of inspiration and hope are as spurs for the inner man.
For the power of life and death are locked up in their roots

And the spoken word can never be retrieved.
So Hawaiians remembered everything.
Their traditions were oral.
Poetry was the answer.
For beautiful words are easily retained in the
*   mind...*
*   And repetition forms a bridge for the memory.*

A deluge of mail swamped the main Post Office in downtown Honolulu. Petitions from all over the Islands were addressed to Queen Liliuokalani. All requested a new constitution. The Hawaiian people were charged with the idea of getting their rights back. They wanted to govern the Islands again. Too much power had been wrested away from them and was now in *"foreign hands;"* namely members of the cabinet and legislative bodies who were not born in Hawaii.

"Give Hawaii back to the Hawaiians!" was the cry.

Later she wrote:*"...To have ignored or disregarded so general a request I must have been deaf to the voice of the people, which tradition tells us is the voice of God. No true Hawaiian chief would have done other than to promise a consideration of their wishes..."*

AINA: *(The Land)*
"The land is a mother that never dies..."

Kaiulani wrote to her aunt Liliuokalani, on the death of her uncle, the news of which had just reached her by cable:

Sundown
Hesketh Park
Southport

Dear Auntie,

I have only just heard the sad news from San Francisco. I cannot tell my feelings just at present, but Auntie, you can think how I feel. I little thought when I said goodbye to my dear Uncle nearly two years ago that it would be the last time I should see his dear face. Please give my love to Mama Moi (Queen Kapiolani), and tell her I can fully sympathize with her.

I cannot write any more, but Auntie, You are the only one left of my dear Mother's family, so I can ask you to do that little thing for me.

I must close with love and kisses,

I remain,

Your loving niece,
Kaiulani
Jan, 21st., 1891.

In September she received a letter from home concerning yet another death, that of her aunt Liliuokalani's husband, John Owen Dominis:

Washington Place.
Sep. 18th, 1891.

My Dear Kaiulani,

You have heard e'er this of the death of your dear Uncle John, from Mrs. Robertson.

I could not write at the time to tell you, for I was so shocked. It all seemed so sudden to me. It is true he had been sick ten weeks but I had no idea he would pass away so soon, for he looked so well that morning. It seems we are having a series of sadness in out family for it is only seven months since my dear brother died, when my husband was taken away - not that only but a short time before Uncle John's death the Queen Dowager Kapiolani had a stroke of paralysis and is likely to have another.

If it is the Father's will in Heaven I must submit for the Bible teaches us "he doeth all things well".

You and Papa are all that is left to me.

I shall look forward to the time when you could finish your studies with all due satisfaction to your teachers, and then come home and live a life of usefulness to your people. My health is pretty good considering all that I had to go through.

On March 9th 1891, Queen Liliuokalani declared her niece, Princess Kaiulani; heir-apparent to the throne of Hawaii.

he Queen soon realized with alarm that sources of revenue were sorely needed by her government. In her frantic search for ways to make money, she supported two very controversial bills; one was to legalize a government lottery and the other was to provide the importation and sale of opium in Hawaii. The *"pillars of the community"* were loud in their criticism of her judgment.

While troubles continued to tax her, throughout 1892, Liliuokalani studied the German language, *"for recreation,"* under the instruction of one Fraulein Wolf. The German teacher was also a *"psychic reader"* who received messages in her cards frequently. Now she began tuning in to the vibrations surrounding the Queen of Hawaii.

A grand ball took place at Iolani Palace on the night of July 7th. Removed from the crowd, huddled in a private corner, Fraulein Wolf sat reading the Queen's cards. Her face was pinched with the intensity of her concentration, as important messages began to come through. Into the early morning hours, as sleepy guests made their way to their carriages, the cards continued to speak, The psychic saw that a man would soon visit the Queen with a scheme to bring money flowing into Hawaii.

True to Fraulein Wolf's vision, soon after, a *"Mr. T.E.E."* whose real identity was never known, called on the Queen at the palace. Of course, the Queen received him, as she was acting under the guidance of the psychic vision. It seemed it was beginning to unfold, as *"Mr. T.E.E."* mentioned the proposal of a National Lottery in presenting himself. The Queen immediately consulted Fraulein Wolf for the next intriguing installment of *"guidance from the beyond."*

The German woman, usually stoic, cried enthusiastically; *"Accept it! It will bring a million and more..."* *"Mr. T.E.E."* was even more grandiose. he promised twelve and a half million over a period of twenty-five years; for rail-roads, bridges, roads, wharves and oceanic cables.

When word of the scheme leaked out to the community, enemies of the Monarchy bitterly opposed it. They saw that it would give the Queen a source of income outside their control.

Burned and thwarted by the raging controversy stirred up by the lottery proposal, *"Mr. T.E.E."* and his friends predicted in disgust that the nation would soon go bankrupt... and certain parties were forcing it, they said... so they could bring forward schemes for annexation.

I n 1892, rumors reached Kaiulani in England that the Queen would appoint Prince David Kawananakoa to succeed her late husband as Governor of Oahu.

Writing from the Davies' family residence that overlooked the Irish Sea, she pleaded with her Aunt: *I hear from many people, that David is to have the Governorship. Please do not think me very forward, but I should so like Father to have it. I have not asked you for anything before, but if you can possibly grant this, I should be so grateful.*

Further on, in the same letter: *When I come home I shall try to help you as much as I can, tho it will not be much as I don't understand State Affairs. Father is going to try to get home as fast as he can, as he may be of some use to you. He was quite unwell last Tuesday. The evening before, he went into the slums of London with a detective, as he wished to see how the police did their work. He did not get home till after one o'clock, so the consequence was he was laid up the next day. The doctor said that the smells had been too much for him...*

Her deep love and concern for her father shows as she pleads further with her aunt:

... I hear that you wish Father to be Governor, but to give up the Customs House. Auntie, we cannot do without his salary for that, as the salary of Governor is only half the other. My education and stay in England is costing him something, and Oh Auntie! I do not want him to get into debt. Please do not be offended with me...

On leaving Great Harrowden Hall...

> *Sundown,*
> *Hesketh Park,*
> *Southport.*

Dear Auntie,

Thank you so much for your kind letter. It is very good of you to write to me, as I know how very busy you must be with State Affairs.

I am so glad to see that Father is putting up a proper house at Ainahau. It has always been my ambition to have a house at Waikiki worthy of the beautiful garden.

I hope that you liked my photographs.

I have left Great Harrowden Hall for good, Mr. Davies has kindly found a lady who will look after, and be a sort of mother to me while I am in Brighton. I believe Mrs. Rooke is a thorough lady.

I shall take lessons in French, German, music and English, especially grammar and composition, I am anxiously waiting for the time to come when I may see you again.

I must close this short letter,
With much love, Believe me,
Your affectionate niece,
Victoria Kaiulani.
Feb. 5th, 1892

Kaiulani was unaware of the trouble that was building up at home between the Royalists and the *"Annexation Club"* which had been secretly formed in 1892.

Dan Logan was now the editor of the Bulletin and he spoke out fearlessly against the *"traitorous sugar barons"* who would see the Monarchy overthrown for their own monetary gain. (Logan was eventually silenced when he was arrested on a charge of libel filed by American Minister John L. Stevens who was a dedicated Annexationist.)

Great tension mounted in Honolulu as the Queen spoke out against her enemies. Concerned for her safety, a group of loyal young Hawaiians led by the six Irish-Hawaiian Lane brothers, appointed themselves round-the-clock guardians of Queen Liliuokalani and took up posts at Iolani Palace.

Minister Stevens' regular despatches to his friend, Secretary of the Navy, James Blaine, were, in part, quite slanderous towards the Queen and those close to her.

On March 8th 1892 he wrote:

"I have information which I deem reliable; that

there is an organized revolutionary party in the Islands This party is hostile to the Queen and to her chief confidants, especially opposed to the coming to the throne of the half-English heir-apparent, now being educated in England..."

He continued:

"The Americans (in the Islands) object to the possibility of an overwhelming English influence in the Government, if the half-English Crown Princess Kaiulani comes to the throne."

Then, referring to Kaiulani's father, Archibald Cleghorn (who was a Scotsman) he said:

"In his younger days, Cleghorn, the reputed father, was no more exclusive in his domestic relations, than was the mother of the princess. Gossip has it that the real father of Kaiulani is an American naval officer from Maine..."

In another despatch in March 1892 Stevens said the Queen was *"losing prestige"* because of her *"illicit relations"* with her Marshal; a half-caste Tahitian named Charles B. Wilson. One passage, that was ordered to be omitted, said: *"It is a general and long-held opinion here, that this man Wilson was for years her paramour, during the lifetime of her invalid American husband who died eight or nine months since..."*

Stevens pointed out that their affair was probably still continuing, for Wilson lived in, or near, the palace, He then gave his opinion: *"The great lack here now is an intelligent and efficient executive, which it is impossible to have, with the existing monarchy..."*

He continued with descriptions of *"the scandal and corruption that has inhabited the palace fir the last twenty years..."*

n March 20th Kaiulani wrote to her aunt from 7 Cambridge Road in Brighton, Sussex, where she was now in the care of Mrs. Rooke:

Brighton is such a nice place, though I have only been here a month, I can find my way about quite easily. I think that I shall profit by my stay here in many ways. The air is very pure and bracing and already my appetite shows me that is suits me.

I am taking lessons in music, singing, literature, history, French and German. I have such a nice lady for a singing mistress. She has taught me such a lot, and she says that I have a very sweet soprano voice - I think that I must have inherited it from you. I am getting on pretty well with my music, and I am so fond of it.

I have enjoyed my studies very much during the last term, and I feel that I am learning something. I can speak German quite fluently, though I make a great many mistakes. I do not feel so very nervous about it as I used to do.

I hope that Father will allow me to stay here till Christmas, then let me travel about on the continent for a month or two before I "Come out" in society.

I am looking forward to my return next year. I am beginning so feel very homesick - I shall be very glad to see you. I suppose that you will not know me again as I have changed so much.

April 19th 1892:

We are starting for Jersey tomorrow, the boat leaves at 12 o'clock at night so we shall have to start pretty early in the afternoon so that we can get comfortably settled.

We go via Southampton. It only takes nine hours to get there, but I believe that it is very rough between Guernsey and Jersey. Mrs. Rooke's house is not very large but her garden is very beautiful. I intend to enjoy my holiday as much as I possibly can, so that I may come back to my studies quite refreshed. We are having very cold weather at the present moment. Last week it was so warm that we all went out of doors without any jackets at all. I must say that I prefer the intense cold to the intense heat.

After a very rough voyage across to Jersey that took two hours longer than usual, Kaiulani was very ill, but managed to write to her aunt:

The drive to St. Helier to Mrs. Rooke's little house at Rozel quiet refreshed me.

On the 26th, still holidaying in Jersey, she wrote:

The weather is quite perfect and altogether this place reminds me very much of home. I wish I was there now. V. K.

Then, written from Brighton:

Last Saturday I had my first lesson in dancing and general deportment which I found highly amusing. My friends tell me that I carry myself so much better when I am walking in the street then in a drawing room, so at the present moment I am doing my very best to walk into a room quietly and gracefully.

My Dear Aunt,

Brighton
May 18, 1892
It is so warm here, I wear white thin blouses all day. They are so very comfortable and cool.

40

The only thing I miss is my riding horse. I would give almost anything if I could have Fairy to ride. Very few people ride here and their horses are so very poor, I would not ride them if they were offered to me.

I am having such very pretty summer dresses made. I like pretty, dainty things. All the ladies are wearing dresses made like men's clothes. I do dislike them as they look so very manly.

> 7 Cambridge Road
> Brighton
> Oct. 25, 1892

My Dear Aunt,

I hope that you will not think me impertinent in asking you for one of your photographs. I have not got one of you.

My room is very pretty but I think a few photos would improve it. At present I have only two - one of Mother and one of Father.

On my birthday Mrs. Rooke gave me "The Soul's Awakening", it is such a beautiful picture. I have always wished to have it, but I never had enough money. It hangs opposite my bed so that the first thing I see in the morning is the girl's lovely face. I received quite a number of presents and such a lot of letters. I spent a very happy day in spite of being such a long way from home.

n January 14th, 1893, Queen Liliuokalani informed her Cabinet Ministers that she intended to form a new constitution which would restore full power to the Monarchy and rights to the Hawaiian people. The Ministers wasted no time in betraying her and scurried downtown with the information to the *"Committee of Safety"*. The *"Committee"* comprised a group of foreign businessmen, mostly American, and was formed solely for the purpose of overthrowing the Monarchy and annexing Hawaii to the United States.

The Queen's Cabinet members were: Samuel Parker; Minister of Foreign Affairs, John F. Colburn; Minister of the Interior, William H. Cornwell; Minister of Finance and Arthur P. Peterson; Attorney-General.

They found another supportive friend in U.S. Minister John L. Stevens who said he feared for the safety of American residents if the Queen were allowed to form the new constitution.

They promptly made arrangements with Stevens, to land marines from the *U.S.S. Boston* in Honolulu upon call. The *Boston* was anchored just offshore and with its huge cannon and well-trained troops, was an ominous threat to this small sovereign nation that depended on a handful of household guards for protection.

The afternoon of Jan. 14th saw the Queen keeping an appointment with her traitorous Cabinet Ministers at 2:30 p.m. in the Blue Room of the Palace.

Outside, members of the Hui Kalaiaina (Hawaiian Political Association), the Household Troops and the Royal Hawaiian Band were all waiting in anticipation.

In the Blue Room, Liliuokalani's Cabinet Ministers talked her out of forming a new constitution.

Sadly she appeared on the second floor verandah of the Palace and addressed her people below.

Speaking in Hawaiian she told them their wishes for a new constitution could not be granted just then, but would some future day...

That promised day never dawned.

Meanwhile the *U.S.S. Boston* slid into the port of Honolulu and plans were made to land a military force, when needed.

All morning, January 16th 1893, the *Committee of Safety* met in Lorrin Thurston's downtown office to make plans for a mass meeting of people in favor of Annexation. Marshal Wilson had the courage to call Thurston out of the room and tell him that the Committee was ordered to disband immediately. In return Wilson promised to make sure the Queen would not indulge in *"any more foolishness"*.

Thurston recalled later that Wilson went on to say:

"I will guarantee that she will not proclaim a new constitution, even if I have to lock her up in a room to keep her from doing it! And I'll do it too if necessary!"

At this, members of the Committee snickered, because all had heard the rumors of *"intimacy"* between the Queen and her Marshal.

AU: *(Time)*
For time is a current flowing through space... revolving... turning over... under and around the earth in a cosmic swirl.

> *As the stars rotate... that is the direction and*
> *motion of time... A daily rotation as "star*
> *lights" pierce the dense darkness.*
> *And relate to the sun as they move from horizon*
> *to horizon.*
> *From sunlight to moonlight.*
> *Time moves through the year and through the sea-*
> *sons from East to West.*

The inner circle of the Annexationists made much of the Queen's attempt to please her people.

"The Committee of Safety's" leader; Lorrin A. Thurston, a local lawyer and grandson of missionaries, called a noisy meeting at the Armory on Beretania St.

Thurston shouted that the Queen had sworn to maintain the old constitution but her word meant nothing... If she had her way, the streets would be red with blood, he added.

Others picked up Thurston's fever. One called out: *"Now is the time to act!"* Another demanded: *"Overthrow this disgusting Monarchy!"*

While this spirited meeting was in progress, U.S. minister Stevens made arrangements to land U. S. troops.

At five p. m. four boatloads of blue-jacketed Marines; a one hundred and sixty man force, scrambled ashore at the foot of Nuuanu Ave.

Throughout all this excitement, revolution or *"the work of the kahunas"* took its toll. Talk spread regarding the kahuna intervention when three leading

Annexationists fell suddenly ill and retreated to their beds. Thurston was one of them.

The Monarchy was hanging on by a thread. The Queen had not yet surrendered. She still had her Royal Guard; several hundred armed men. The Annexationists had about half the number. But support from the newly arrived U. S. Troops tilted the balance.

PULE: *(Prayer)*
For in the philosophy of old Hawaii...
Everything was preceded by prayer
And the way was then cleared for progress...
And their major beliefs were so similar to those taught by the visitors...
Treat others as you would be treated yourself...
And never hurt another by thought, word or deed... for the act will return to you...

HUNA: *(Secret)*
And the kahunas were "Keepers of the Secrets"...
Priests who were trained experts in many fields...
Some were healers and could diagnose illness at a glance
Some were astronomers
And some were astrologers
And they read the shapes of clouds or the positions of stars
And some were weather forecasters who guaged the moods of winds and seas
And some were navigators who guided mighty canoes across vast stretches of uncharted ocean...
All were prophets or seers...

ollowing their successful mass meeting on Jan. 16th, the jubilant Committee of Safety felt sure that the Queen's abdication was imminent.

They met at 7:30 that night at the home of Henry Waterhouse, to form a new government. Their choice of an executive for the new regime was Sanford Ballard Dole; an American Justice of the Supreme Court. (Dole was born in the Islands of American parents.) Until now he had taken no active part at all in the movement against the Queen. He said he still felt it was not quite the right time to do away with the Monarchy. But he had to admit that he thought Hawaii's destiny lay with the United States, as Liliuokalani had now clearly forfeited her throne. A regency for Princess Kaiulani would be the best immediate solution, he said.

After Wilson left, Archibald Cleghorn came to plead for the cause of his absent daughter. He suggested to Lorrin Thurston that, if the Queen were to be deposed, then Princess Kaiulani; the heir should be appointed Queen and rule under the guidance of a Board of Regents. Things would be greatly improved from what they had been, he pointed out. Thurston answered coldly, matter-of-factly that it was too late to consider any of this. Things had gone too far. He and his colleagues wanted no Monarchy at all.

The Committee of Safety nodded and approved of every word Thurston said in reply to Cleghorn's plea.

The aging Cleghorn was quite heartbroken as the realization began to sink in: his daughter's birthright was to be swept away forever. He bowed his grey head and retreated down the stairs, looking as if he were about to weep.

46

That same afternoon, a British sympathizer called on the Queen herself and begged her to *"abdicate at once"* in favor of Princess Kaiulani whom *"the people adored."* Such action could save the failing Monarchy, he said.

But Queen Liliuokalani was stubborn. She refused. Thinking that her situation would improve, she held on.

The Committee of Safety was wasting no time. About three o'clock during the cloudy afternoon of the next day, Tuesday, January 17, a wagonload of their arms and ammunition rolled out of a store on King Street.

A native Hawaiian policeman, Leialoha, rushed forward, grabbed the horse's reins and tried to climb on the wagon. He was promptly shot in the fleshy part of his shoulder by the driver of the wagon, John Good.

As the day wore on, an anxious crowd had assembled in Palace Square to await further developments in the tense situation. At the sound of the single shot from John Good's gun, the crowd, joined by alerted members of the police force, ran towards Fort and King Streets. The Committee of Safety was delighted. It was a perfect diversion, clearing the way for them to carry out the final phase of the revolution. They hurried to Aliiolani Hale; the Administrative Building on King St.

One Committee member, Henry E. Cooper, was the messenger who had alerted the commander of the *U.S.S. Boston* to be ready to bring troops ashore. An American who had only arrived in the Islands the previous year, Cooper was doing very well for himself. Now, his duties increased, he announced that the Monarchy was *"abrogated."* then, coughing into his fist with the excitement of it all, he raised his head again and proudly went on to say: *"A Provisional Government has been established until terms of a union with the United States have been negotiated and agreed upon..."*

Beside the Committee of Safety members, there were few witnesses to the reading of such a momentous document. Seventeen year-old William Soper had run there in search of his father, John Soper, Commander of the Committee's Military Forces. A few clerks working inside the building couldn't believe their ears when they heard what was happening.

Most of Honolulu's population were simply unaware of what was taking place. U.S. Minister Stevens duly recognized the *"new government"* and so notified the Queen. Martial Law was then declared in Honolulu and an order issued that all other arms must be turned in.

A new power had taken over the Government Building. In their own way, the Queen's changeable Cabinet Ministers appeared to be rallying around her at the eleventh hour. But their motives were always in doubt. At the Police Station, they drafted a note to U.S. Minister Stevens ridiculously asking his assistance in this appalling situation.

They wrote that they had *"... been informed that certain persons to them unknown have issued proclamation declaring a Provisional Government... and having pretended to depose the Queen, her Cabinet and Marshal, and that certain treasonable persons at present occupy the Government Building in Honolulu with an armed force, and pretending that your excellency, on behalf of the United States of America, has recognized such Provisional Government, Her Majesty's Cabinet asks respectfully, has your excellency recognized such Provisional Government? And if not, Her Majesty's Government under the above exciting circumstances respectfully requests the assistance of your government in preserving the peace of the country."*

The note was delivered to the American legation about 2:45 p.m. Minister Stevens' daughter received it saying that her father was *"very unwell"* and unable to reply just then. Later the Queen's Cabinet Ministers insisted that they were ready to put down any revolt, but were hampered by Stevens' delay.

At 5 p.m., a delegation called on the Queen at Iolani Palace demanding she surrender. Samuel M, Damon of the Committee of Safety's Advisory Council warned her that if she resisted there would be bloodshed... a great many would be killed... probably including herself.

As darkness began to fall, Queen Liliuokalani surrendered. With armed U.S. Marines patrolling the streets, she saw the futility of resistance. Also, she firmly believed that once the U.S. Government learned the facts, she would be re-instated. She signed a document, yielding not to the revolutionaries, but to the *"superior force of the U.S.A., whose Minister Plenipotentiary, His Excellency John L. Stevens, has caused U.S. troops to be landed at Honolulu and declared that he would support the said Provisional Government..."*

The Queen's Marshal, Charles Wilson, gave up the Police Station, while over at the Barracks, her Hawaiian troops stacked their rifles for the last time. The sun had set on the Hawaiian Monarchy. A handful of businessmen had succeeded in toppling the throne.

That night, Honolulu was rocked by the strongest earthquake ever recorded in the Islands. Talk flew that Pele was outraged at what had taken place.

The Monarchy was no more.

AHI *(Fire)*
And the deity of Pele was the one most feared and respected.
For she was the exciting Queen of fire, the Goddess of volcanoes
And she visited each of the Islands in turn... leaving flames in her wake.
And she often appeared to travelers on lonely roads
As an old woman wearing a black holoku
With a small white dog walking beside her...
Or a carefree young woman with auburn hair blowing in the wind and wearing a flame red dress.

The Queen prepared the following document for the PGs:

I, Liliuokalani, by the grace of God and under the Constitution of the Hawaiian Kingdom, Queen, do hereby solemnly protest against any and all acts done against myself and the Constitutional Govt. of the Hawaiian Kingdom by cer-

tain persons claiming to have established a provisional government of and for this Kingdom. That I yield to the superior force of the United States of America whose Minister Plenipotentiary, His Excellency John L. Stevens, has caused the United States troops to be landed at Honolulu and declaring he would support such a provisional government.

Now to avoid collision of armed forces and perhaps loss of life, I do, under this protest and impelled by such forces, yield my authority until such time as the Government of the United States shall upon the facts being presented to it, undo the action of its representative and reinstate me in the authority which I claim as the Constitutional Sovereign of the Hawaiian Islands.

Done at Honolulu this 17th day of January, 1893.

Judge Hartwell was the last witness to leave the room. He shook the Queen's hand with tears welling in his eyes. Mrs. Wilson, the Queen's lady-in-waiting, scoffed as he left: *"Crocodile tears."*

The Queen wrote later:

After those in my place of imprisonment had all affixed their signatures, they left, with the single exception of Mr. A.S. Hartwell. As he prepared to go, he came forward, shook me by the hand, and the tears streamed down his cheeks. This was a matter engaged in a righteous and honorable action, why should he be affected? Was it the consciousness of a mean act which overcame him so? Mrs. Wilson, who stood behind my chair through-

out the ceremony, made the remark that those were crocodile's tears. I leave it to the reader to say what were his actual feelings in the case...

Badly shaken by the takeover, Cleghorn wrote his opinion of the Queen's actions to Kaiulani:

It is the first time in 16 days I have called. I had called once before but her people said she was resting - as a rule I try to visit her once a week.

Since the 17th January I have no pleasure in talking with her, as she is to blame for all our troubles.

Has she written you since the 17th Jan,? If not please say so in your answer to this.

He wrote further:

If the Queen had abdicated the night of the 16th or early on the 17th, the throne I think could have been saved. But she did not think they would do as they did, she still followed the advice of poor Ministers' wretched wills, and we have all to suffer.

I visited her several times that day, 17th, and told her there would be a provisional government. Still she held on - and one hour after, the Committee called and told her they had the Government in their hands, To have resisted would have cost a lot of lives, and made things worse.

On February 1, 1893, Minister Stevens proclaimed a United States Protectorate over Hawaii which would not *"... interfere with the administration of public affairs by the Provisional Government..."*

The stars and stripes now flew over Aliiolani Hale, replacing the Hawaiian flag. Deposed Queen Liliuokalani could not bear to look at it when she drove by in her carriage. She wrote in her diary: *"Time may wear off the feeling of injury... but my dear flag... the Hawaiian flag... that a strange flag should wave over it! May Heaven look down on these Missionaries and punish them for their deeds..."*

The Queen could do nothing more now than retire to her private residence, Washington Place, and wait for the United States to act. She had yielded only to that power; never to the Provisional Government, condoned by Minister Stevens and his cronies. Very quickly, this new government became the butt of jokes and ridicule in many quarters, as people tried to get used to the idea of a new rule. They were widely referred to by a shortened version of their title... simply, *"the PGs."*

HO'OMAU: *(To continue or renew.)*
Hawaiians have an awareness of the journey right through to the beyond... the state after death. Generation followed generation...
And some moved out into the light as they floated and circled silently... ever rising on the ascending spiral...
And their consciousness grew and expanded according to the lessons of life.

ight from the time he arrived in Hawaii, 73 year-old U.S. Minister John Leavitt Stevens allied himself with the Annexationists. He had been dubbed a *"rabble-rouser"* by newspapers in his home state of Maine where he had first been a Minister of the Gospel, then a newsman, then a politician. His latest ambition was to become a power in Hawaiian politics.

Expressing his views in an article he wrote for the *Kennebec Journal* on November 17, 1892, the year prior to the overthrow, Stevens said:

"The time is near when we must decide who shall hold these (Hawaiian) islands as a part of their national territory. It is not possible for them much longer to remain alone. Their people and the United States will soon be compelled by circumstances and events to decide whether the Hawaiian Islands will have sanity, liberty and autonomy with the United States, or become a colonial possession of a European power..."

Queen Liliuokalani later wrote of Minister Stevens:

"Several times in my presence, to which he had access by virtue of his official position, he conducted himself with such a disregard of good manners as to excite the comment of my friends.

His official despatches to his own government, from the first days of his landing, abound in statements to prove (according to his view) the great advantage of an overthrow of the monarchy, and a cession of my domains to the rule of the United States."

Within a few days of the overthrow a news report reached Honolulu regarding Minister Stevens' only daughter Ann who also served as his secretary.

Princess Kaiulani 1875-1899

Kaiulani in her 11th year.

Left to right: Annie Cleghorn, Paymaster: Mr. Hind, A.S. Cleghorn and
his daughter Kaiulani at Ainahau, 1887.

King Kalakaua.

She drowned off the coast of the Big Island, as boatmen tried to put her ashore from an inter-island vessel. Soon it was discovered that she had been gathering names for a petition to annex the Islands to the American Union. Rumors flew that the loss of her life was a punishment against Stevens, organised by the kahunas.

On January 18, the PGs decided to send five commissioners to Washington to arrange a *"quick annexation"* of the Hawaiian Islands.

To counteract this move, Liliuokalani sent attorney Paul Neumann and Prince David Kawananakoa to defend the Monarchy on her behalf.

In England on Jan. 30th, 1893, Kaiulani's guardian Mr. Theophilus H. Davies received three telegrams. One said, *"Queen Deposed"*; the second read *"Monarchy Abrogated"*; and the third asked Mr. Davies to: *"Break News to Princess."*

Kaiulani was stunned. Mr. Davies suggested that Kaiulani make an immediate trip to Washington to plead Hawaii's case with the newly elected President, Grover Cleveland. He and his wife would accompany her.

Meanwhile, Kaiulani's uncle, John Cleghorn, her father's brother went racing across the continent to Washington where he would press his niece's claim to the Hawaiian throne. He lived in San Francisco and the San Francisco Chronicle found it very amusing to watch his race with the Annexation commissioners who were also on their way. Who would get there first? They asked their readers regarding *"the most novel and important long-distance race in American history."*

Kaiulani, in her 18th year, was still shy of the political world. At first she said she couldn't face such an ordeal but, on thinking it over, she decided: *"Perhaps someday the Hawaiians will say that Kaiulani could have saved us but she didn't even try! I will go with you."*

In February, Princess Kaiulani issued a statement through the London newspapers which read:

Four years ago, at the request of Mr. Thurston, then a Hawaiian Cabinet Minister, I was sent away to England to be educated privately and fitted to the position which by the Constitution of Hawaii I was to inherit. For all these years I have patiently and in exile striven to fit myself for my return this year to my native country. I am now told that Mr. Thurston is in Washington asking you to take away my flag and my throne. No one tells me even this officially. Have I done anything wrong, that this wrong should be done to me and my people? I am coming to Washington to plead for my throne, my nation and my flag. Will not the great American people hear me?

A friend wrote to Kaiulani:

I read in the Bulletin that you are going to Washington to do all you can for the Monarchy's cause.

Do take care, Dear, as I feel that some enemies of your family would stop at nothing at this point. We all feel something is coming to a head here at home. Everyone is so worried. We Hawaiians can scarcely put our heads out the door anymore, for fear of being accused of something. The PGs are so suspicious! They're always sniffing out "Royalist plots" even when there are none! One day they'll have a real one on their hands...

few days later, the Princess sailed from England for the United States on the *Teutonic,* accompanied by Mr. and Mrs. Davies, their daughter Alice, a chaperone and a maid.

Arriving March 1st in New York harbor, Kaiulani had prepared a statement which she read to the newspaper reporters and hordes of people who swarmed over the pier for a glimpse of the Princess who might become an American citizen if her homeland were annexed:

Unbidden I stand upon your shores today where I had thought so soon to receive a royal welcome. I come unattended except for the loving hearts that come with me over the winter seas. I hear the Commissioners from my land have been for many days asking this great nation to take away my little vineyard. They speak no word to me, and leave me to find out as I can from the rumours of the air that they would leave me without a home or a name or a nation.

Seventy years ago, Christian America sent over Christian men and women to give religion and civilization to Hawaii. Today three of the sons of those missionaries are at your capital, asking you to undo their fathers' work. Who sent them? Who gave them the authority to break the Constitution which they swore they would uphold?

Today, I, a poor weak girl, with not one of my people near me and all these statesmen against me, have strength to stand up for the rights of my people. Even now I can hear their wail in my heart, and it gives me strength and courage and I am strong... strong in the faith of God, strong in the knowledge that I am right, strong in the strength of seventy mil-

lion people who in this free land will hear my cry and will refuse to let their flag cover dishonour to mine!

Critics in Honolulu laughed at the Princess' appeal saying that Mr. Davies wrote every statement she made, while mainland newspaper accounts published the next day glowed with descriptions of Kaiulani. One said:

"The Princess is a tall beautiful young woman of sweet face and slender figure."

Another wrote: *"The Princess impresses one as tall and slight with decidedly good eyes which are soft brown. Her hair is almost black and somewhat wavy. Her complexion is dark but not more than many girls whom one meets every day on Broadway."*

During her brief visits to Boston and Washington, writers continued to enthuse, writing that *"whenever Kaiulani passes through hotel dining rooms, comments of admiration are heard on all sides."*

The Provisional Government, or the *"PGs."*, as they became scornfully known, were very watchful of any newspaper reporters who wrote articles against them. It was also forbidden to agree with any mainland newspapers who spoke out against those *"usurpers in Hawaii ..."* They put a *"gag law"* into effect. The first to be arrested under it was John Sheldon, the editor of *Holomua,* which had been the Queen's own paper. Sheldon was charged with *"contempt of the Government."*

Carson Kenyon, an Englishman who replaced Sheldon, also criticized the PG's policies. He, too, was thrown into a dirty basement in the jail.

Then came Edmund Norrie, a Dane, as the new editor of *Holomua.* He was to become the most outspoken of all against the PGs. *"Who is for Annexation?"* he asked his readers. Then replying to his own question: *"Certainly not the Hawaiians. And of the eighteen hundred Americans in the Islands, less than half favor it..."*

Meanwhile, talk circulated that this pet subject of the PGs - Annexation - was *"imminent."* That was their next step. They also boasted that their Annexation Club was now spreading *"Island wide."* Thinking erroneously that its membership would be overwhelming, they were disappointed to gather fewer than seven hundred signatures. Many of those were extracted under threats of people losing their jobs if they didn't sign up.

Losing no time in moving to their next plan, the PGs had announced on January 18 they were sending a delegation to Washington to ask for Annexation.

It was on hearing this, that the Queen immediately prepared to send her lawyer, Paul Neumann; Prince David Kawananakoa and Edward C. Macfarlane, her ex-Finance Minister, to act on her behalf in Washington. (Prince David was the late King's nephew, his wife's sister's son.)

As the ship *Claudine* was about to sail for the mainland the Queen's representatives were astonished when they were refused passage on her. (The *Claudine* was owned by local planters.) So their arrival in Washington was frustratingly delayed, while they waited for another ship. The PGs had well and truly presented their case, by the time the Queen's party arrived.

The president said that from the time the Annexation of Hawaii was suggested he was *"utterly and constantly opposed to it."* He considered it *"opposed to national policy"* and furthermore *"it perverted the mission of America..."* At noon on March 9, 1893. Cleveland withdrew the Hawaiian Treaty from the Senate. Secretary of State Gresham declared: *"It would lower our national standard to endorse a selfish and dishonorable scheme to acquire title to the Islands by force and violence..."*

Visiting Annexationists Castle and Thurston were furious and stormed into Gresham's office demanding an explanation. They were told that the Cleveland Administration had insufficient facts and knowledge of the whole subject of the Treaty... and for that reason it had been withdrawn.

Finally, on March 13, 1893, Princess Kaiulani was received at the White House by President Grover Cleveland and his wife, who was popularly known as *"the White House Bride"*. Twenty five years younger than her husband, the President's wife was greatly loved by the American people.

Kaiulani later commented on how *"sweet and beautiful"* Mrs. Cleveland was and added that the President was *"entertaining"*.

The mention of politics was carefully avoided, but President Cleveland managed to convey to the princess that he meant to see justice done to her and her country. Kaiulani also hoped to counteract some of the vicious propaganda written by the PGs in which they accused Hawaii's rulers of being *"undisciplined savages."*

Still the visiting PG Commissioners were pushing as hard as they could for the Annexation Bill to pass.

Lorrin A Thurston, W.R. Castle, C.L. Carter, W.C. Wilder and J. Marsden - all spoke up passionately for Annexation.

In Hawaii, just seventy years before, the ancestors of the white government members were a meek band of missionaries, newly arrived from New England, with little or no money in their pockets. The Bible was their prime possession. They came to convert the heathen.

"Bow your heads in prayer," they told them, while it was natural to a Hawaiian to look upwards to the stars which he knew gave him life in the first place. Many went to their graves, broken in heart and spirit, having been told everything they stood for was wrong.

One young planter, whose grandfather was in the First Company of Missionaries and whose father was now a millionaire, stated confidently: *"We don't want a 'picturesque' government. We want a government under which we can make money!"* It summed up the attitude of the oligarchy in the mid-1890s.

Copy from *The Mail* and *Express Bureau* in Washington, D.C., on March 8, 1893, read:

The Princess Kaiulani arrived this morning from Boston. The train was late and although she was due at the Arlington at 10:30 o'clock, she did not arrive until after 12. There were very few to receive her, but Prince David was on hand to welcome his fiancee.

The Princess looked tired after her journey. She was dressed in a dark travelling costume and a big broad blue hat. Around her neck was a garland of La France roses and smilax reaching to her waist. As she entered the Hotel with Mr. and

Mrs. Davies, Prince David rushed to the front door and shook her by the hand. The Princess was at once shown to her apartments on the second floor.

What will be done officially in presenting her case to the State Dept. has not been decided. The Hawaiian Annexation treaty is not dead. Unless President Cleveland shall withdraw it from the Senate as he did the Nicaragua Canal treaty soon after he entered the Presidency in 1885, it will continue 'alive' for action by the Senate at the pleasure of that body. There are many Senators here who say the Princess has hurt her own cause by coming here. Mr. Cleveland has been silent so far in regard to his feeling toward the question, but it is thought before many days he will bring the matter before the Senate again.

While visiting Washington Princess Kaiulani was interviewed by one Mr. S.E. Moffett. His story appeared on the front page of the San Francisco *Examiner* on March 19, 1893. She refers to her former life in Hawaii which she left when she was thirteen:

"My favorite occupation was riding. I liked to mingle with the natives... especially of the lower classes. I was with them so much more than with persons of higher position. They are such an affectionate, generous, simple people, that it was a pleasure to be in their company."

"They were always just as glad to see me and to give me whatever they had that was good to eat..."

Theophilus Davies mentioned to reporters: *"Over Wormley's Hotel where the Provisional Government*

Commissioners are stopping, I noticed this morning, gentlemen, that the Hawaiian flag is flown. Yet I am told that the American flag flies over the Honolulu Government Building. A curious state of affairs!"

When Kaiulani arrived in Washington, Prince David Kawananakoa was already there working with Paul Neumann (the deposed Queen's lawyer). In a gallant effort to combat the distorted picture of the Hawaiian Monarchy that was deliberately painted by the PGs and to regain the throne for Liliuokalani, Kawananakoa told reporters that *"it seemed that Kaiulani was influenced by Mr. Davies in coming to America."* The Prince stated further: *"Mr. Davies is working against the interests of the Queen, which is in bad taste to say the least."*

Despite his disapproving attitude, Prince David made a courtesy call on Kaiulani at Brevoort House in New York where she and her party had rented suites.

But, as Kaiulani and Mr. and Mrs. Davies had heard of his remarks regarding their visit, he was only allowed to talk to the Princess for a few minutes, and that at 10 o'clock at night when he was finally admitted to her suite at the tail-end of a stream of callers.

Regardless of the rift that existed between Kaiulani and Kawananakoa, the newspapers still feasted on their imagined engagement, one reporting that the Princess' *"fiance"*, Prince David, was waiting to greet her on her arrival in New York.

On the same morning of Kaiulani's visit to President Cleveland, he announced that he would send a special investigator to report on the situation in Hawaii. By his receiving Princess Kaiulani, he underscored his sympathy towards the plight of the Hawaiian Monarchy. The PG commissioners were furious, as the President's appointment of an investigator would now hinder their well laid plans to rush Annexation through *"as quickly as possible, with no questions asked."*

Washington papers were full of speculation both for and against Annexation: after all, American property interests in Hawaii were now very great. Rumors buzzed about as they tried to guess whom the President would appoint as his personal investigator.

On March 15, Mr. Davies, ever loyal to Hawaii, addressed the public regarding the situation:

> *One of the saddest features of this matter is that it has been presented as a plot and a conspiracy of bad men. It is not that. It is the blunder of good men, men to many of whom I would entrust my dearest interests. They have been goaded on by misrule into injustice, forgetting that injustice is not remedy for misrule. Today the Provisional Government of Hawaii dares not appeal to the Electorate to ratify any one of their acts, What kind of Government is that?*

Within a couple of days, President Cleveland announced that ex-Congressman James H. Blount of Georgia was to sail immediately for Honolulu, and make a full report on the situation there. The President also conferred on Blount paramount authority over any other American official in the Hawaiian Islands. He quickly became know as *"Paramount Blount"*.

Signing herself only as *"C.K."*, a Royalist family friend wrote to Kaiulani:

"The kahunas foresaw all this! Oh. Kaiulani, that's the saddest part of all to me..."

In the meantime we'll see what we can do here to change things. We're not finished yet. A strong and growing group of us are constantly trying to restore the Monarchy and the rights of the people. My uncle and his friends are working "on another level," you might say. More with the forces of old Hawaii. They can see many things beneath the surface, and that is where they direct their prayers; to undermine the roots of it all.

So try not to worry.

"C.K." wrote further:

The kahunas are prosecuted under the law now, so they have to be very careful of their activities these days. All our people still go to them in times of illness, though.

HO'OMANA: *(To worship)*
Then the people of the Islands felt the eternal need to make their souls and nature's soul into tangible things... to be seen and felt.
And always warshipping the mystic force of nature...
The Hawaiians personified its aspects.
And so the Gods were born.

"Paramount Blount" said later that, while being interviewed for the appointment to Hawaii by the President and Cabinet, he got the distinct impression that Cleveland wanted *"authentic information,"* in-

stead of the distorted reports that had been filtering through to Washington. Secretary of State Gresham seemed to want no less than to see the U.S. flag lowered in Honolulu.

James Blount, his ailing wife and a stenographic clerk, Ellis Mills, sailed on the U.S. Revenue cutter *"Rush"* from San Francisco on March 20, 1893. They arrived March 29. Meanwhile, Lorrin Thurston and colleagues C.L. Carter and W.R. Castle raged to the head of the PGs, Sanford Ballard Dole, that President Cleveland had been cursed with a *"suspicious disposition"* and had never supported their *"course of action."*

Two days after he arrived in Hawaii, Special Commissioner Blount ordered the American flag to be hauled down from Aliiolani Hale; the American troops were to return to their ship and the protectorate ordered by U.S. Minister Stevens (without authority) was to be withdrawn immediately. The house-cleaning had begun.

As the Hawaiian flag rose again on the Government Building, a crowd of Hawaiians came to watch in silence.

It seemed to Kaiulani that America had finally come to care about the fate of her Islands and before she and the Davies family returned to England where she was to continue her studies for an indefinite period, she issued a farewell statement to the American Press:

> *Before I leave this land, I want to thank all whose kindnesses have made my visit such a happy one. Not only the hundreds of hands I have*

clasped nor the kind smiles I have seen, but the written words of sympathy that have been sent to me from so many homes, have made me feel that whatever happens to me I shall never be a stranger to you again. It was to all the American people I spoke and they heard me as I knew they would. And now God bless you for it - from the beautiful home where your fair First Lady reigns to the little crippled boy who sent his loving letter and prayer.

During her entire visit newsman enthused in their descriptions of Kaiulani: *"delicate beauty, with exquisitely small, well shaped hands, an accomplished musician, an artist, a linguist with the genteel manners of a born aristocrat."* The derogatory comments spread by the PGs regarding the Monarchy began to appear somewhat ridiculous and most leading American newspapers now became very outspoken in their support of the Royalist cause.

A few newspapers remained distinctly pro-Annexation, energized by the picture the PGs had painted. But the influential New York Times called for a *"complete investigation"* in the Hawaiian Islands, while the St. Louis Chronicle said the revolution in Hawaii was not *"by the people but by those who were not permitted by Queen Liliuokalani to plunder the land."*

Harper's Magazine spoke strongly against Annexation and the *"tricks"* of the PGs while the New York Herald flatly stated: *"Mr. Thurston's threat to deliver the Islands to England if the treaty is not ratified, is not quite nice."*

Constant harassment by the press in Hawaii continued as the *Pacific Commercial Advertiser* in April of 1893 published a story telling readers that, *"ex-Princess Kaiulani is really engaged to be married to a son of Theo. H. Davies. The young gentleman in question, Mr. Clive Davies, is now studying in Boston. It is well known that Kaiulani was often a guest of Mr. Davies in his home in Southport, England, and the prospect of the union would account in some measure for the extraordinary zeal lately displayed by Mr. Davies on behalf of the ex-Princess."*

The rumors of the *"engagement"* had probably been fanned by Kaiulani's visit, the month before, to Boston's Institute of Technology where young Clive was studying. (She was accompanied by Clive Davies' parents.) The Princess instantly charmed the young men in Clive's class at the College, many of whom were so smitten that they followed her to other appointments around the city.

Meanwhile, her father, at home at Ainahau, repeatedly and sometimes gruffly, denied the rumored romance. *"There is not a word of truth in it!"* Cleghorn said. *"It is absurd!"*

S oon after the Queen was dethroned, a great gathering of kahuna took place on Oahu; master kahuna, healers, praying kahuna and those possessed by special gods. All shared the opinion that the Hawaiian people had committed a great sin and the loss of their throne and government was its consequence.

The people were reminded of the ancient prophecy: When the Hawaiians turned their backs on gods and aumakua, thereby forfeiting their help and protection, strangers would come from overseas and possess their land…

All the kahuna at the great gathering, now prayed for a sign of the atonement needed to restore the Queen to power.

Three women kahuna simultaneously received the same answer to their prayers in a trance state; human sacrifice must be made if the Queen were to be restored.

The three women walked to Washington Place to see the Queen. They proposed that they should walk in procession with the Queen and enter the Palace gates on King St.

"Ma kou mamua (we in front) ke alii mai mahope (you behind)... and we will stop the mouth of the cannon", they said.

The women predicted that the PG soldiers and their guns would be powerless, once the kahuna marched, chanting with their Queen up to the palace.

Once inside the throne Room, they would lead the Queen to the throne, seat her on it... then they would die.

If death did not come at once, it would in a few days... and the Queen would know the gods had accepted their sacrifice.

But Liliuokalani refused to carry out the plan of the kahuna. She feared the ridicule of haoles and soldiers at the palace if the plan failed. *"The revolutionists would consider it so much native superstition and heathen practice,"* she said.

Although some said she was never entirely satisfied with her Christian beliefs, and was always seeking, still her faith in the old gods was too shaken, for her to ask them for anything.

n May 17, Minister John L. Stevens was brusquely recalled from his post in Hawaii. He wasn't too upset, as he had already mailed his resignation to Washington, and announced his departure as *"the end of May."* He moved from the American Legation to the Eagle Hotel where, on the eve of his departure, he was cheered and saluted in the hotel grounds by at least five hundred members of the Annexation Club who had brought a band with them. They presented their *"eloquent old man"* with a silver service. His *"work"* in Hawaii was finished. (Barely two years later, Stevens died at his home in Augusta, Maine.)

When Stevens departed Liliuokalani wrote: *"Mr. J.L. Stevens went back to the United States on the steamer Australia with a history which has never been paralleled in Hawaii... May be he made to suffer as much as the many pangs he has caused among the people..."*

Cleghorn kept Kaiulani faithfully informed of developments at home and in a letter, written in May, he said:

> Blount is a busy man taking in all, in regard to our troubles. I have not had a talk with him yet. I think I wrote you that I called on him the day after his arrival, but the Captain of the Ship was present, so I did not talk politics - What his upset will be here, who knows for he never gives anyone any idea of his plans.

> Spreckels and his family are here and he is opposed to Annexation, but a friend of his told me he wanted a Republic, and that would be better than Annexation to the States, at least I think so.

Again from Cleghorn in 1893:

Mr. Blount the Commissioner from President Cleveland is hard at work processing all the information he can. I have not had a talk with him yet. He paid your Aunt his first visit yesterday. he was coming out of Washington Place as I was going in.

May 11, 1893

L.A. Thurston has been appointed by the PG as Minister to Washington. He will work all he knows for Annexation. The papers here are very annoying. They do write such nasty articles. We have one in particular the Star. That paper was started for the Annexation Club and they do write such nasty things. I spend long days at Ainahau...

On the 24th of May, the Queen wrote to Kaiulani informing her that she was to be offered the Throne:

My Dear Kaiulani,

I simply write to assure you that we are well. Papa seemed in good health but I think looks a little thin.

I hear from some parties that your house is looking fine, but Mr. Robertson says he has not ever seen it.

Kaiulani's aunt continues with the real purpose of the letter:

I would simply like to add and say that should anyone write or propose or make any proposition to you in any way in regard to taking the Throne, I hope you will be guarded in your answer. The people all over the Islands have petitioned to have me restored and it would make you appear in an awkward light to accept any over-

tures from any irresponsible party, and the PGs
are growing less and less, and I understand they
will soon drop to pieces as the saying is, for want
of funds to carry on the Govt. Mr. Spreckels will
not help them or loan them any money and Bishop
and Co. would not loan them any money without
Mr. Spreckels - and now we are waiting patiently
till the U.S. Commissioner in Mr. Stevens' place,
could tell us we are free. I will write you and ac-
quaint you of all that transpires, and if need be
will advise you after consulting with your father.

Later, on June 1st, Liliuokalani writes apologiz-
ing for the above *"hurried note"* as she was getting
ready to receive a young Indian Prince, the Nawab of
Kampur. She said that as the Prince was leaving he
remarked to some Hawaiians: *"Why did her people*
permit her to be deposed?"

The Queen explained:

Come to think of it, my dear Kaiulani, it was
treachery on the part of my Ministers.(and it
helped the agitation backed by the U.S. troops) -
that was why, but don't mention this. It would
not be well if it came from your lips - we have to
act with policy.

Kaiulani replied to her aunt from the Yews,
Kettering:

I have never received any proposals from any-
body to take the Throne. I have not received a
word of any sort from anyone except my father. I
am glad that I am able to say that I have not writ-
ten to anyone about politics.

I have been perfectly miserable during the
past four months. I have looked forward to '93 as

being the end of my "exile". I have considered the four years I have been in England as years of exile. Now is seems as though things would never settle and I am simply longing to see you all - People little know how hard it is to wait patiently for news from home. Mr. Davies is very kind and sends me all the information he can, but I suppose we shall not get any real news as to the settlement of affairs for months. In the meantime, "il faut attendre."

I am staying with my old school mistress Mrs. Sharp. She gave up her school (Great Harrowden Hall) two years ago, and is now living in a dear little home of her own.

I am as happy as I can possibly be under the circumstances.

I am really and truly recruiting my health which has not been good lately.

I do a good deal of hard reading, practicing, sewing and gardening.

While *"Paramount Blount"* was busy gathering evidence for his report to Washington, his friend, reporter Charles Nordhoff, who reached Hawaii April 7, was sending despatches to the New York Herald Tribune which showed the American public an entirely different picture of the situation in Hawaii. *"All Hawaiians are against Annexation...,"* Nordhoff wrote. *"Only the planters favor it."*

The San Francisco Argonaut responded with the statement: *"America is not in the business of robbing foreign nations of their lands."*

While still in office, Minister Stevens had lost no time reporting to his friends in the Provisional Government that the outspoken Nordhoff was conspiring with the Royalists to oust them (the PGs). Charles Nordhoff, meanwhile, endured threats of violence and libel suits because of the articles he wrote.

Plots against Queen Liliuokalani abounded at this time. The PGs were constantly looking for ways to frame her… then have her deported. Her presence in the Islands was a nuisance to them.

On May 30. a bundle of explosives was found buried, close by the barracks of the PGs. Of course, the Royalists were blamed. But after a thorough investigation into the matter by Commissioner Blount, they were freed from suspicion.

Later, the militant Royalist newspaper Holomua extracted a signed confession from a PG policeman named A. Juen who admitted he had been ordered to plant the explosives and throw suspicion on the Queen and her followers so *"Liliuokalani would then be deported by the PGs."* On June 2, the PGs moved into Iolani Palace and re-named the elegant structure the *"Executive Building."* Their order were that it was never again to be referred to as *"the Palace."*

Cleghorn kept Kaiulani informed:

June 19, 1893

I have nothing to write that will please you. The PGs have moved into the Palace which I think is a shame, but I hope the day is not far distant when they will have to go out for good - things look better, still we do not know what the U.S. Govt. will do.

I cannot make out what the end will be. I do

not think we will be annexed, still there are a great many working against the Monarchy. A Republic would be worse than Annexation. I am in hopes that Mr. Blount will do what is right, and Mr. Cleveland has the reputation of being both an able and upright man.

June 21, 1893

We heard yesterday from a sailing visitor that Thurston has been accepted as Minister from Hawaii by the President. I was rather in hopes the U.S. Govt. would not receive him - still they may not have been able to do otherwise.

June 29. 1893

Spreckels will leave and I hope will go on to Washington. He is strong on our side and will do all in his power for the restoration of the Monarchy.

By August 8, 1893, Commissioner Blount had completed his report on the situation in Hawaii and was returning to Washington.

A huge crowd of Hawaiians came to the wharf to bid farewell to Blount and his wife, who boarded the ship with flower leis stacked around their necks.

The PG band also turned out to bid farewell to the departing *"President's Man"*, but their attitude was vastly different from the *aloha* of the Hawaiians.

The Provisional Government had firmly adopted *"Marching Through Georgia"* as their theme song and, delighted with their choice, they used every opportunity to play it.

Now they lustily struck up their favorite tune, apparently considering it an appropriate (but not very subtle) insult to *"Paramont Blount"* who was a former officer in the Confederate Army.

On reaching Washington, Blount reported to the U.S. Senate that *"A great wrong has been done to the Hawaiians, who are overwhelmingly opposed to Annexation."* He suggested that *"their legitimate government should be restored."*

President Cleveland subsequently asked Congress to *"devise a solution consistent with American honor, integrity and morality."*

The PGs began a newspaper called the *Star,* edited by Dr. J.S. McGrew, a physician of Honolulu, who was widely known as the *"Father of Annexation".*

Cleghorn wrote on August 23:

> *The newspapers here are simply dreadful. The Annexation Club is printing the most bitter things about us. I am glad you do not see the Star....*

James Blount's official report reached Secretary of State Gresham in early August. It recommended that the Senate *"...right the wrong done to a feeble but independent state... by restoring the legitimate government. Anything short of that will not satisfy the demands of justice. Our government should be the last to acquire sovereignty over them, by force and fraud..."*

Two clear facts emerged from Blount's voluminous findings: firstly, the commissioner found that former U.S. Minister Stevens, backed by American forces, had aided in the overthrow of Queen Liliuokalani Secondly, he noted that if the question of annexation were put to a popular vote amongst the people of the Islands, it would lose by a margin of *"at least two to one..."*

Secretary of State Gresham was impressed by articles on the Hawaiian question, written by Carl Schurz, editorial writer for *Harper's Weekly*. His most celebrated piece was entitled: *"Manifest Destiny,"* in which he pointed out how history had shown that Anglo-Saxon democratic institutions could not survive in tropical colonies. He wrote: *"If attached to the United States, Hawaii would always retain a colonial character. No candid American could ever think of making a state of the Union out of such a group of Islands..."*

In mid-September, after he had studied the Blount report, Gresham wrote to Schurz: *"I can say to you in confidence that if anything can be established by proof, Mr. Blount's reports show that the action of the American Minister and the presence of the United States troops in Honolulu overawed the Queen... put her in fear... and induced her to abdicate and surrender to the so-called Provisional Government with the understanding, however, that her case would be fairly considered by the President of the United States. Should not this great wrong be undone? Yes, I say decidedly. Aside from the President and Cabinet, this is more than I have said or written to anyone and you will understand the importance of not allowing this letter to fall into other hands..."*

Queen Liliuokalani wrote: *"At this time men were going about town with firearms; shots were at times flying about the city, whistling through the air, or penetrating houses to the great danger of the occupants; and no one was responsible for the local disorder.*

Words of harm towards my person had been openly spoken by the revolutionists; spies were in my household, and surrounded my house by day and by night; spies were also stationed at the steps of the Congregational Church opposite my residence, to take note of those who entered my gates, how long they remained, and when they went out. My respect for true religion prevents my stating the active part one of the preachers of God's word took in this espionage. It was under these circumstances that I prepared to visit Mr. Willis in accordance with his request..."

The Queen was soon to meet with Albert S. Willis, the new Minister to the United States.

The Provisional Government did everything to tighten its control. Many young Hawaiians were thrown out of their jobs because they chose to remain loyal to their Queen.

The *Bulletin* Wrote in praise of them: *"All of them are honest and capable..."* The six Irish-Hawaiian Lane brothers were mentioned in particular for their unwavering stand against the PGs. *"All honor that the inquisition has thus far developed is reflected in the many young Hawaiians who have been its first victims. They could have saved their positions by practicing the duplicity of many others... and promising to carry a gun against their friends and kindred. These young men retire with the respect of the whole community... leaving it for the inquisitor and his colleagues to suffer the pangs caused by loss of self-respect."*

With Stevens removed, a new U.S. Minister was appointed.

Albert S. Willis arrived in Hawaii November 4, 1893, with instructions from President Cleveland to inform the Queen that she might *"...Rely on the justice of this government to undo the flagrant wrong... However, at the same time, inform her that when reinstated, the President expects that she will pursue a magnanimous course, granting full amnesty to all who participated in the movement against her..."*

But Liliuokalani did not feel magnanimous towards those who had betrayed her. She was wary and cautious as she replied: *"To grant amnesty is beyond my powers as a constitutional sovereign. I could not act without the consent of my ministers. Those who are guilty of treason should suffer the penalty of death and their property be confiscated by the Government..."*

In his notes, Minister Willis substituted the word *"beheaded"* for the Queen's words *"penalty of death"* He duly reported back to Secretary of State Gresham, then arranged a second interview with the Queen. He read the statement back to her, *"from notes of the former interview."*

Liliuokalani wrote later, *"Had I held the document in my own hand and been permitted to read it, I would have noticed the clause: 'my opponents beheaded.' That is a form of punishment never used in the Hawaiian Islands either before or since the coming of the foreigners."*

During the second interview with Willis, Liliuokalani still insisted on the penalty of banishment for those involved in the overthrow. *"There will never be peace in the Islands as long as they remain here,"* she said.

Many thought the new U.S. Minister Willis made an honest effort to carry out President Cleveland's instructions to: *"...undo the Revolution and restore Liliuokalani to power."*

But it was already too late. The PGs dug their heels in and refused to give up.

Conditions worsened for the Hawaiian people. Homesteaders living on lands given to them by the Queen were now threatened with eviction, unless they signed the oath of allegiance to the PGs. This time, Sanford Ballard Dole, who had long been *"caught in the middle,"* intervened on the Hawaiians' behalf. He assured them that he would personally prevent the loss of their lands. Letters to the Bulletin had called on Dole to show: *"his real self again."* One writer addressed him directly: *"You have been loved by Hawaiians and respected by haoles. We cannot believe you are so greatly changed..."*

On September 12, Kaiulani wrote to her aunt from the Yews:

> *My Dear Aunt,*
> *How you must hate the sight of the Central Union Church. What a shame that a house of worship should be turned into a spy tower. I suppose it is wiser for you to remain at Washington Place, but how you must long to get away to some other place. If I was in your place, I am afraid I should pine away and die - I could not stand it - I am so tired of waiting—*

By the time this reaches you it will be my birthday. I hope that you will remember me away from my relations and friends.

In a tense Honolulu, soldiers were billeted in both Central Union and Kawaiahao churches.

Kaiulani expressed her worries to her aunt:

I am getting to be quite a good needlewoman, Now things have gone wrong, my money matters are in a muddle. I am sure I do not know what I shall do if the PG don't give me some money. We were never very well off - I have to make $500 a year buy everything I need except my food and lodging - I have never been in debt till now.

I will try and be cheerful but I am so homesick! There is no disguising the fact.

Before U.S. Minister Willis arrived in Honolulu, Annie Cleghorn wrote to Kaiulani:

Well Kaiulani dear, from all accounts it seems as though your Aunt will be restored.

She has behaved remarkably will through all the insults that have been heaped upon her. She has been blackguarded right and left. I hope she will remember those who rejoiced and helped in the overthrow. They always professed to be great friends of Royalty.

We have no American Minister here at present. I expect the next one will bring the news.

November of 1893 saw much unrest in Honolulu following attempts to restore Liliuokalani to the Throne. Her life was threatened many times.

To Kaiulani from her aunt, November 6, 1893:

You may understand how much your father and I had to go through, but there is nothing like being self-possessed and you ought to practice it. Think before you say or act and keep cool at all times. It has been the means of guiding my actions through all these nine months and from all I hear has had a good effect on the people that no blood has been shed, and will end in good results for us. Patience and endurance will always have its reward. I have not much time to write as everything around us seems to be in commotion. The American Minister calls on the PG this morning at eleven - will present his credentials. His name is Willis. He and wife and son arrived last Saturday by the Australia. He is the one who holds our future destiny in his hands.

Meanwhile the Bulletin asked its readers, *"What is a PG, since they are neither American nor Hawaiian?"*

he year 1894 dawned in a Honolulu gripped by an atmosphere of tension and suspicion. Many were *"spied on"* for showing the slightest hint of disloyalty to the PGs. The organist at Kawaiahao Church was arrested on little more than *"suspicion of disloyalty,"* while another German resident was pulled in for saying *"Damn the PGs!"* in public. A luau at the Waimanalo home of John

Cummins was raided as it *"appeared to be a Royalist meeting"* ...and even the chapel of the Seventh Day Adventists was raided. Finally, all large gatherings were forbidden by the jittery PGs.

In her writings, the Queen gave a glimpse of the trusting nature of the Hawaiians: *"Although it is generally conceded all over the world, and common sense would seem to show how one should act towards one's enemies, yet there was the strongest intermingling of those of the two parties, which were called the 'Royalists' and the 'PGs'. Instead of recognizing each other as enemies, and keeping apart as such, they associated as in former days. Visiting went on just the same, exchanges of thought and opinion were the same. The Royalists, open-hearted and free of speech, socially ignored the fact that the PGs were, in every material sense, their enemies. These latter kept the situation in view, and with soft words studied to worm out of the unsuspecting all that they could in the way of information as to Royalist hopes and plans, that the particulars might be communicated to the PG Government..."*

Meanwhile, *"other voices"* in Honolulu were clamoring to be heard. Although most opinions on the mainland seemed to simply divide the *"problem of Hawaii"* as between Hawaiians and haole missionaries, there were other races to be considered; races that had been over-looked by the *"Reformers"* in their zeal to get rid of the Monarchy. They had been brought in as field hands on plantations, but many had *"bettered"* themselves by 1893 and had acquired businesses in Honolulu.

Now they demanded their *"rights."* They were

interested in who governed the Islands, too. The Japanese had become ambitious and opened up shops in town. The Chinese had followed the same pattern some years before. The Provisional Government now tried to curb the enterprise of these Orientals by saying they could only enter into trade and business with their consent. Loud protests ensued. The Portuguese immigrants chose to support the Provisional Government, right from its inception in 1893. They even joined the PGs Armed Forces with their own *"Volunteer Company C."*

Early in the year, the Provisional Government announced plans for a day-long celebration of its first anniversary in January, 1894. *"What are they celebrating?"* asked Editor Dan Logan of the Bulletin. *"They have glutted themselves with mean revenges. They have a four million dollar debt and a standing army of idle men and spies..."*

The threat of trouble about to erupt, hung over Honolulu like a tangible cloud, lingering... full of portent.

Everyone was being spied on for the slightest hint of disloyalty to the PGs and every luau by Hawaiians was suspected of being a *"Royalist meeting."*

By this time, many foreigners who had formerly supported the PGs regretted the overthrow of the Monarchy and detested the suspicious nature of the government that now reigned in its place.

HOPOHOPO: *(Uncertainty)*
And the limits of time settled over them like confining shrouds
And an unknown anxiety cramped their spirits

For now they felt they were hastening towards a
death where they would be judged...
Even for "sins" with which they were born.
And they were Children of Nature no more.
For they were trapped by these Holy Jugglers of
People's Lives
And like drowners clinging to slender reeds
They held fast to the last traces of their old be-
liefs
Lest the mouth of time swallow them up forever
And they drew on all their inner creativity to de-
vise means of preservation.

The PG leaders made many changes to existing laws. Soon, they realized it would also be
wise to get rid of the word *"provisional"* in their title.
After all they were the government now!

On March 15, 1894, they called a convention to
draft a constitution for their new title: *"The Republic
of Hawaii."* On July 4, Sanford Ballard Dole announced its inauguration and proclaimed himself
"President."

The same day, Liliuokalani wrote in her diary:
*"What matters if they do set up their Constitution and
establish a Republic? When the U.S. is ready, she will
undo all that her Minister has done..."* But the Royalists were getting restless. They wanted to know ex-
actly what the President of the United States intended
to do about the Hawaiian Islands.

Finally, the Queen arranged for a delegation of
three to journey to Washington and find out first hand
what hope still existed for her restoration. John
Cummins, Judge Herman A. Widemann and Samuel

Parker sailed on July 13. Major William T. Seward accompanied John Cummins as his secretary.

After waiting for two weeks to see President Cleveland, they received instead a letter from him delivered to the Arlington Hotel. It read in part: *"...Quite lately a Government has been established in Hawaii which is in full force and operation in all parts of the Islands. It is maintaining its authority and discharging all ordinary governmental functions... and it is clearly entitled to our recognition without regard to any of the incidents which accompanied or preceded its inauguration, This recognition and the attitude of the Congress concerning Hawaiian affairs of course leads to an absolute denial of the least present or future aid or encouragement on my part to any effort to restore any government heretofore existing in the Hawaiian Islands..."*

Once in control. *"The PGs"* demanded that everyone sign an *"oath of allegiance"* to them.

Rather than sign, the Royal Hawaiian Band boys all resigned. Their bandmaster Henry Berger told them they would starve if they did not earn a living and they would be forced to eat stones...

One of the bandboys replied they would be proud to eat stones; all that was left to them; mystic food of their native land.

Local composer Ellen Prendergast (Kekoaohiwaikalani) was so moved and inspired by the bandboys' loyalty that she composed the song of rebellion: *"Mele Ai Pohaku"..."The Stone Eaters Chant"*

The first verse moved everyone who heard it:

Kaulana na pua a'o Hawai'i
Kipa'a mahope o ka 'aina
Hiki mai ka 'elele o ka loko 'ino
Palapala 'anunu me ka pakaha.

Famous are the flowers of Hawaii
Ever loyal to the land
When the evil-hearted messenger comes
  With his greedy document of extortion.

Reeling from the terrible news that kept reaching her like a dark stream, Kaiulani in England, wrote to Mary Gaines, a friend in Ireland:

I feel such a pull from the Islands in this time of trouble for my people. I often cry for my far islands... and I swear I can hear something calling back to me. Is this normal I wonder?

They are as living things to me... as real as relatives. Oh, I do hope justice and goodness prevail and my people are able to hold the nation together. They don't deserve what's happening...

"C.K." Wrote to Kaiulani; an account of a Royalist ceremony with ancient roots:

As all gatherings are now forbidden to us, we have devised methods of passing along information or sometimes just to give ourselves hope for our cause. Uncle says we Hawaiians have always been poets and masters of allegory.

Recently your aunt gave a large piece of her land as a park in Pauoa Valley. We all decided to carry out the planting with formal Hawaiian ceremony as in the old days. Uncle supervised everything. The park is to be called Uluhaimalama

*which of course means to us: "as the plants grow
upwards from the dark earth towards the light:
so will light come to our nation,"*

*As usual, suspicious PG Police patrolled the
streets leading to the park... spying on everything
we did! I was so moved when the first small group
of Hawaiians arrived for the morning ceremony.
They were led by our own National Band which
the boys formed, after resigning from the Royal
Hawaiian Band, rather than play for the PGs who
took that band over. What a scene it was, V.K. I
wish you could have been there. Each Hawaiian
wore a hatband with lettering in gold, spelling
out Ulu-hai-malama. They kept coming from all
directions. My heart was bursting with love for
our people that day!*

*At nine a.m. the band played the National an-
them. Many people were crying, as your Koa
(Prince David) planted a sapling of the lehua tree
which is. as you know, much loved by the Queen.
Then an old man, Nalani, chanted to her: "This
is the Heavenly One! May the gods protect her as
she protects her people..."*

*Other trees and shrubs were then planted
around the lehua to symbolize the circle of the
love with which the people surrounded their Monarch.*

*Nalani chanted on: "The kukui... a light for
your government. The hala polapola... your favorite lei, O Heavenly One... sweet to inhale. The
pilimai: the love of your people clings to you.
Cling fast to your land... your people... your
throne, Oh Our Queen!"*

Then a very ancient ritual followed... A single stone had been placed on top of a small mound of earth. It was a symbol of the creation of the earth. The old chanter's voice rose as he praised the land; the true mother of all...

Many loving hands then patted the soft earth surrounding the stone, and so many Hawaiian tears fell into that soil. Then the people sang the Stone Eaters Chant: "Mele Aloha Aina; Song of The Land We Love."

Oh, Kaiulani, something great and eternal in our people will live on, I know it. I have faith in their mana!

In England, Kaiulani told a friend:

... Last night I dreamt I heard my peacocks crying in the night. So plaintive and lost they sounded. I awoke with my throat aching, because I couldn't let my feelings out...

With Royalist circles buzzing with plans for armed revolt, Herman Widemann made one last attempt at easing the situation through diplomacy. He asked John Bush for help in gathering as many native signatures as they could put on a petition which asked the Queen to send an envoy to the great powers of Europe. Perhaps they would aid the Hawaiian Royalists' cause. Via Washington, Widemann went on the mission himself, paying his own expenses. All Hawaii waited. The impatient Royalists waited. But Judge Widemann had no good news to send back from Europe. Everywhere he went, he was refused official reception. The Republic of Hawaii was widely recognized now, as the established government. The PGs were winning.

The Queen wrote in her journal:

"At the time of the return of Mr. Widemann from abroad, the intensity of the feeling was at its height amongst the Hawaiian people that something should be done to save their country. Of their own accord, they bought rifles, pistols and other arms, stealthily keeping these for future use...

"Many who swore allegiance to the "Republic of Hawaii" began to regret bitterly that they ever permitted themselves to support the revolutionary party. They had been in comfortable circumstances, had even laid aside for a rainy day, and felt that the savings of their years of prosperity would find them independent in life's decline. But since the overthrow of honest government they had lost, or been forced to spend, all they had accumulated, and the little business left to them would scarcely sustain their families.

Weary with waiting, impatient under the wrongs they were suffering, preparations were undoubtedly made amongst some in sympathy with the monarchy, to overthrow the oligarchy... If they were now by one accord, determined to break away, and endeavor, by a bold stroke, to win back their nationality, why should I prohibit the outburst of patriotism? I told them that if the mass of the native people chose to rise, and try to throw off the yoke, I would say nothing against it, but I could not approve of mere rioting..."

Unofficially, Secretary of State Gresham remained on the side of the Monarchy's cause, even encouraging the Royalists to fight for its restoration, if they had to. The investigative party, sent by the Queen, returned to Honolulu on Thursday, August 30.

Word had reached them... on Aug. 27... that President Cleveland had: *"recognized the Republic of Hawaii."*

With disappointment, the Royalists realized that Cleveland had been forced to abandon their cause. The mounting pressures became too great for his party as they prepared for elections in the fall. Meanwhile, letters of sympathy for the fallen Monarchy poured into Hawaii from all over the United States. Some people even offered to come over and *"fight for the Queen."*

President Cleveland was ousted in the fall elections and McKinley went into office.

In Honolulu, the Royalists were gathering arms for a clash with the government that had taken over their land. So many felt that it was useless to talk anymore with those in power. They had nothing left but to fight.

When Kaiulani was five years old, her uncle King Kalakaua had visited Japan on his trip around the world in 1881. It was a trip designed to declare Hawaii a sovereign nation amongst the other nations of the world and it also made him the first King to circumnavigate the globe.

His Majesty was very impressed with the manners and appearance of a fifteen year old Prince whom he met at Japanese training school where young men were rigorously prepared for military careers.

Komatsu was a nephew of the Mikado, Emperor of Japan, and the political possibilities of an alliance between the Prince and Kaiulani loomed in Kalakaua's mind.

On impulse, the Hawaiian King sought a private audience with the Japanese Emperor and, after a formal tea ceremony at the Imperial Palace, he proposed the future marriage of the two young people.

In wanting to unite the Thrones of Hawaii and Japan, Kalakaua foresaw that Japan's powerful navy would make an impressive ally in the defense of his tiny Kingdom against usurpation by other nations, and especially America, whose citizens in Hawaii already had too much control of the economics and politics of Hawaii.

On the other hand, the islands were strategically placed in the Pacific for coaling and trading purposes and offered fresh land for homesteading and commercial pursuits.

The conversation continued between the two rulers with many veiled allusions to all of the benefits of such an alliance.

The Emperor's countenance was stoic as he neither declined nor accepted, but pointed out that Prince Komatsu was already betrothed, hinting, however, that engagements can sometimes be broken.

(After Kalakaua's return to Hawaii, the proposal was politely declined in a letter from Prince Komatsu himself who regretted that he was already betrothed.)

Thirteen years later, when Queen Liliuokalani was desperately searching for support in her fight against

Annexation, she wrote of the proposal to Kaiulani who apparently had not heard of it before.

In a long letter written from Washington Place, the Queen spoke of both Kaiulani's and Hawaii's future.

My Dear Niece,

Your father called the other day and kindly handed me your note, and I am so glad to hear from you. It is true that many reports have been circulated in the newspapers about my restoration, and in fact many thought it was already settled, but many causes arose that prevented its immediate accomplishment, but I suppose you will have read of it by this time and everything connected with our situation by the President's Message to the Senate and Congress. The delay is unfortunate but the President has said the wrong must be righted, and so it will have to be as according to my protest, everything has been sifted by able men specially appointed to investigate our affairs and their statements have proved satisfactory that the "Queen has done us wrong, but that the American Minister Stevens has done a great wrong." So my dear child we are only waiting for the "good news", then you may come home. It has been a weary waiting and everybody seems disheartened almost with the waiting. Business is dull, no money circulating and those who have it will not spend because of the present government - as everything done now is illegal and it would be a loss to them or parties venturing to spend.

You have asked me a direct question and I must be candid with you in regard to Prince David.

I had not thought of mentioning to you about your future until the proper moment arrived but as you already mention it, it is best you should marry one or the other of the Princes, that we may have more aliis. There are no other aliis whom they (the people) look to except Prince David or his brother who would be eligible to the Throne, or worthy of it, and they turn to these two aliis that there may be more aliis to make the Throne permanent according to the Constitution. To you then depends the hope of the nation and unfortunately we cannot always do as we like, in our position as ruler and which you will have to be some day, in some things our course and actions will have to be guided by certain rules and which could not be avoided, I am pleased to see your candor in regard to Prince David - It is good to be candid.

The last part of the Queen's letter discussed the Japanese Prince:

I have to mention another matter, one which I think you ought to know and I hope you will write at your earliest chance and inform me what your opinion is in this matter. When your uncle, the late King was living, he made arrangements that you should be united to one of the Japanese Princes. He is the nephew to the Emperor of Japan. It seems that the young Prince was here in the Naniwa on her first trip last year, but our position was such that he could not present himself, so I have not seen him, I understand now that the Prince is in England being educated so you may meet him on your return. I do not know his name but should you meet him and think you could like

94

him I give you full leave to accept him, should he propose to you and offer his hand and fortune. It would be a good alliance. They speak highly of his qualities. And now do not hesitate to open your heart to me. I shall be very glad if such an alliance could be consummated between you two and I shall look forward for a letter from you with eagerness, saying it was agreeable to you, and that will encourage his suit. Do not wish to get fat. If you could only see me you would not wish to be. I have grown almost as stout as Kahuila Wilcox. I am pleased to know that you have a lady with you whose society is pleasing to you. I hope she will come out with you. The above must be between you and I and not mentioned outside until such alliance could be consummated between you two, and of course you can write me. then it does not matter if it goes abroad.

Your affectionate Aunt,
Liliuokalani
Washington Place, Jan, 29, 1894.

It took Kaiulani five months to reply to her Aunt:

10 Beaumont Street, London W.
June 22, 1894.

Dear Aunt,

It is a very long time since I received your kind letter, I have often tried to answer it, but have failed, I have thought over what you said in it about my marrying some Prince from Japan.

Unless it is absolutely necessary, I would much rather not do so.

I could have married an enormously rich German Count, but I could not care for him. I feel it would be wrong if I married a man I did not love. I should be perfectly unhappy, and we should not agree and instead of being an example to the married women of today I should become like them, merely a woman of fashion and most likely a flirt. I hope I am not expressing myself too strongly, but I feel I must speak out to you and there must be perfect confidence between you and me dear Aunt.

I have been looking anxiously every day in the papers for news from home, but nothing seems to have happened. I wish things could be properly settled. It is such weary work waiting here not knowing what is happening.

The course of Hawaiian history might have been quite different if Kaiulani had received a proposal from the Japanese Prince.

Apparently. King Kalakaua and Queen Liliuokalani strongly believed that a marriage between Kaiulani and Komatsu could have been advantageous to both Hawaii and Japan and would have established a Japanese Protectorate over the Hawaiian Islands. As the clouds of Annexation gathered ominously, the Japanese Government would have aided Hawaii in her struggle to remain free.

Still deeply disturbed by the bad news that kept reaching her from home, Kaiulani wrote to her aunt of her travels in Germany in mid 1894:

> *I was quite sorry to leave Germany, everyone had been so very kind to me there, and they have sympathized with us so much. During the last month of my stay in Germany I went to Berlin and there I saw the grand Parade before the Emperor and Empress. It was really a sight worth seeing, there were nearly twenty thousand soldiers and the Emperor had a staff of 100 officers.*

> *Berlin is a most interesting City, it is much more beautiful than London as streets are so wide and most beautifully kept. I visited all the palaces of the Emperors.*

> *Frederick the Great's Palace of Sans Souci I cared least for; it was built after the style of Versailles. He was a very great admirer of the French.*

> *Potsdam where the Emperor stays when he is near Berlin is a most lovely spot about 10 miles miles from it. It is on the borders of two lakes and all around it is quite wooded. All the best regiments are stationed there and it is altogether a very sweet place.*

Always pleased to talk to someone about home, Kaiulani wrote of a visit by Mr. and Mrs. Walker. He was the British Vice Consul to Hawaii, and Mrs. Walker was one of Kaiulani's travelling companions when she sailed from Hawaii in 1889.

> *Mr. and Mrs. Walker came to see me day before yesterday. I was so pleased to see them. We*

had such a good talk about Honolulu. She was very much astonished to find how very tall and slight I am, as she always imagined me stout as I was when I was a school-girl. I am leaving London on Tuesday to visit Mrs. Sharp and then I go to the Davies family for most of the summer.

At the approach of the holidays she wrote to Aunt Liliuokalani from Southport:

…I must just write you a few words to wish you a Merry Xmas and a Happy New Year. This is my sixth Xmas I have spent away from my home, it seems as if I were fated never to come back.

Concerned about her aunt's recent trouble with her eyesight Kaiulani sympathized:

I know well what it is to suffer from the eyes. Sometimes now if I look very long at anything I get such a headache I don't know what to do.

A description of Kaiulani by a friend in the mid 1890s:

Animated, capricious, headstrong, yes but her vivacity had a certain quiet sadness. Her eyes were too large above cheeks flushed hectically; but such pride of bearing, love of companions and heart-felt loyalty of feeling for her native Hawaiians.

From Honolulu, *"C.K."* wrote of an upsetting incident:

The other evening all the family came over. Auntie Winona and her children; their husbands and wives; two of Mama's older sisters and a lot of other friends. Well, you know these Hawaiian gatherings… such warmth and good food and music and fun. Each of the older women… and their men, got up and did their own personal version of the hula. Some were very funny. Auntie Win is a comedy in herself.

Suddenly, she door burst open... our front door which opens right into our large living room. Then four soldiers from the PG guard pushed their way inside and pointed their rifles at us! The children screamed. Papa moved quickly to stand in front of Mama and me. My brother Kimo stood in front of them and asked what they wanted. And do you know V.K. one of the soldiers hit him in the chest with his rifle butt and knocked him out of the way! "All gatherings of Hawaiians are forbidden by the Government!" the leader shouted at us. He was a mean looking fellow with a smirk on his red face. His eyes went all around the room. On the mantel-piece we always have that lovely framed picture of you. Do you know he went over and picked it up and smirked at it. We thought he was going to take it, but he put it down again, because I was glaring at him all the while. "This looks like a Royalist meeting to me, i'll be putting that in my report... along with your names," he said. Then he proceeded to make a list of everyone in the room.

Well, we all got the fright of our lives.. Poor Auntie Winona had to lie down and so did Mama, after the soldiers left, needless to say, that was the end of the ;party. An innocent get-together by our own family! Oh, Kaiulani what have our lives become here? It's getting unbearable. Something has to be done...

he beginning of 1895 in Honolulu was hot with secret plans for imminent rebellion. Even foreigners were *"fed up"* with the PGs.

In late November, 1894, Major William T. Seward, a former American Army officer and friend of John Cummins (he had accompanied Cummins to Washington earlier in the year) had gone to California and bought arms and ammunition. It was rumored that the Spreckels family paid for them. but it is closer to the truth to conclude that Royalists of wealthy background in Honolulu all donated towards the cause.

The arms were shipped to Honolulu on the schooner *Wahlberg* which landed on windward Oahu the night of December 30,. Under the cover of a dark, moonless sky, the cache was transferred to the coastal steamer *Waimanalo* whose captain, William Davies, was a devoted Royalist.

The *Waimanalo* rendezvoused off the Diamond Head home of Henry Bertelmann on January 3, 1895. The Royalists were to launch their first attack that night, but their ranks were overly enthusiastic as they assembled by the hundreds at the Honolulu harbor waterfront.

The suspicions of the ever-watchful PG Police were aroused. They sped to the noisy gathering. Many Hawaiians were arrested… some were severely beaten.

Currently on the side of the monarchy, the changeable Robert Wilcox rode at full gallop towards the Bertelmann home at Diamond Head where the steamer *Waimanalo* lay offshore. Leaping from his sweaty horse, Wilcox paddled a canoe out to the dark ship to warn Captain Davies that the harbor was now under heavy guard by the PGs.

Most of the guns and ammunition were then carried ashore and buried in the sand at the foot of Diamond Head, crouched like a huge guardian lion in the darkness. Some of the arms and shells were planted in the home of newspaper editor John E. Bush and more in Queen Liliuokalani's fragrant garden at Washington Place on Beretania St. The Royalists were ready to fight for their Queen.

On the night of January sixth, the PG Police, strained and jumpy with continued rumors of a Royalist uprising, searched through Waikiki, looking for hidden guns. The PG patrol. led by Captain Robert Parker, was joined by Charles Carter and two of his friends who tagged along enroute, *"just for the fun of it."*

As they scouted the Diamond Head area, they were fired on from the dark shadows around Henry Bertelmann's house. Carter began to lag behind, making grunting noises through clenched teeth. Then his heavy body fell clumsily into the shrubbery. Blood spurted from gaping wounds in his shoulder and abdomen. As the PG party fired furiously back, two Hawaiian Royalists were shot. They bled profusely from chest and leg wounds and lay unattended on Bertelmann's lawn. A PG courier was promptly despatched to Honolulu to enlist reinforcements for their side.

Charles Carter died the next morning from his Royalist-inflicted wounds. A report published by the anti-Royalist newspaper The Star called him: *"a martyr for the cause..."* and mentioned that he was one of the five Annexation Commissioners who had hastened to Washington in 1893.

News of the flare-up at Bertelmann's house spread like wildfire throughout Royalist circles. The PGs were now shooting on sight any stragglers who had taken part in the fighting that killed Charles Carter. The tired Royalist rebels headed for refuge on the massive sides of Diamond Head. A PG tugboat anchored offshore fired its cannon at them as they moved like ants through the greyish bracken. They were attacked from land and sea.

Tired and outnumbered, the Hawaiians were beaten and lay wounded and dying on the slopes of Diamond Head.

After this uprising, more than a hundred Hawaiian Royalists were thrown in jail and on January 16, almost two years to the day from the time she was asked to abdicate, Queen Liliuokalani was placed under arrest. She was always a threat as long as she was free.

She was taken into custody at Washington Place then driven under guard to Iolani Palace where she was imprisoned.

She later wrote: *"My crime was that I knew my people were conspiring to throw off the yoke of the oppressor."*

The Queen also wrote that, after being arrested, she glanced back through the window of the carriage that drove her away and saw Chief Justice Judd of the Supreme Court entering Washington Place.

A local newspaper printed the following item: *"While the rebels fought for days on the barren slopes of Diamond Head, without proper food or drink to sustain them, one Hawaiian woman took her place fearlessly beside the men. She only put her rifle down and took time off once: to bake a dog for the starving men to eat. It was her own pet."*

At Iolani Palace the Queen was led, under guard, to a suite of a bare upstairs rooms; airy, but uncarpeted. A small bed stood in one corner.

A week later, her Marshal of the Kingdom, Charles Wilson, brought her a document of complete abdication, prepared by the Provisional Government and their lawyers. The Queen reluctantly signed, hesitating as she wondered which name she should use. She was told: *"Just plain Liliuokalani Dominis..."* Her title meant nothing to them. Writing later of those dark days, the Queen said she hoped: *"... by signing this paper... all those who had been arrested... all of my people now in trouble by reason of their love and loyalty towards me... would be immediately released. The stream of blood, ready to flow, could be stayed by my pen..."* But some blood had already flowed. Some lives were already altered forever.

All of the Queen's personal retainers and servants at Washington Place were also thrown into prison. They later told of their outrage as they watched the Chief Justice rummaging through the Queen's private papers, her bureau drawers and her safe until he found her diaries. He then began to read them until. feeling the scornful eyes of the staff on him, he stuffed the books into his pockets and left the house.

The following account of her arrest and imprisonment is from *"Private Memoranda of the Queen,"* dated March 4, 1895, Iolani Palace:

"At 10:00 a.m. of Wed. the sixteenth of Jan. 1895, I was occupied in my bedroom. Mrs. Wil-

son, who had just come in, notified me that Deputy Marshal Brown and Capt. Waipa were coming up the front walk. I told her to show them into the parlor and soon followed her.

"On my entrance, before I had a chance to speak, Mr. Brown told me that he had been sent to serve a summons on me, holding up a paper which he held in his hands, and never delivered to me up to this day. He went on to say that I must accompany them. it took me a few minutes to get ready. In the meantime, Waipa had followed me to my room, followed by Mrs. Wilson, Mrs. Clark, Milaina Wakaki, J. Heleluhe and others.

"Waipa said, while tears streamed down his cheeks, that he never thought that he would be the one to have to perform such an unpleasant duty on my person… that of arresting me. (Were they crocodile tears?) He said Mrs. Clark was to accompany me. After bidding my ohuas goodbye, I entered Mr. Brown's carriage and with Waipa drove out of Washington Place."

"Quite a crowd of people had gathered in front of the Central Union Church to see my departure and more were coming with sad countenances and tears. We turned down Richard St. while in my mind I wondered what they were going to do with me. A few minutes brought us to Kinau Gate and we turned into the Palace grounds."

"As we drove towards the Palace, I saw a number of soldiers lying on the grass near tents on the ewa side of Kauikeaouli Gate, in uniforms, with guns either stacked, or by their side… every

man with cartridge belts ready to spring at a moment's notice. Our carriage stopped at the mauka steps of the Palace and I was told to alight. Capt. J.H. Fisher very politely stepped forward and offered his hand, which I took and he lead the way. I noticed Mr. W.C. King pointing his camera at us and have since seen the picture in the Examiner. With Mr. Fisher and Brown and Waipa ahead, we mounted the long stairs..."

During these times of conflict, heroes emerged, such as Irish-Hawaiian Lot Lane. With his handful of rugged Royalists, he was the last to leave the steep battleground of Diamond Head. Some of his men were badly wounded, as they hacked their way through the green tangle of Manoa valley. Wild PG bullets flew around them. They passed many small homes in the area, where Hawaiian and Chinese Valley residents brought them whatever food and water they could spare.

Lot separated from them and went back up the mountain alone. He was shot at and tracked by bloodhounds before he reached the lookout spot he sought. For three days he remained, high on a mountain crevice. Then he noticed that all firing had ceased in the city below. He rushed down, thinking that the promised foreign aid had, at last, been given to the Hawaiian cause. But a friend met him, enroute. His dark face was streaked with bitter tears. The man could barely mouth the words: *"Our Queen was arrested today. Most of our friends are in jail too,"*

Lot replied that he must join his comrades. His friend warned that the PGs might shoot him on sight. But Lot strode off.

Unshaven, barefoot and ragged, he presented himself at the PG Police Headquarters. *"I'm Lot Lane,"* he announced. With the most sought-after fugitive standing before them, The PGs on duty were undecided how to handle his arrest. He was a giant, this one, and might be a bit rough to handle. They fidgeted with papers on their desks. Then one became the spokesman: *"We demand to know the names of those who helped the Hawaiian cause!"* But they got nothing from Lot Lane.

Eventually he was hustled off, by six guards, to a dingy room where more than a hundred starving, forlorn Hawaiians were lying or squatting on the floor. One thin young boy with the distinctive Kainoa features etching his face sat in a corner by himself. Blood was caked on his forehead and matted his hair. Kimo Kainoa had decided to join the rebels at the last minute. He caught up with stragglers from Lot's group. as PG bullets drove them deeper into Manoa Valley. But Kimo merely slowed down the path of a PG bullet as it grazed the side of his head. It was too late to fight.

On seeing them,, Lot went berserk. he knocked over a stack of tin plates with a loud clatter and demanded food for the men. Frightened PG guards mumbled that it was *"too late at night..."* But Lot roared again, demanding food. Meat and poi were

Liliuokalani on the say she was proclaimed Queen: Jan. 30th, 1891.

Provisional Govt. officials.

At Iolani Palace: The arrest of Queen Liliuokalani, Jan. 16th 1895.

Princess Kaiulani, on her way back home. Nov. 1897.

brought to them.

On the day the trials of the *"traitors"* began, the Throne Room, the make-shift courtroom was filled to capacity.

The loyal Royalists filed in: The six Lane brothers, a ruggedly good-looking group; and intense-faced revolutionary Robert Wilcox, who could never quite decide on his cause. With his head held high, the alii entered: Prince Kuhio, the brother of Koa (Prince David). then came Anglo-Hawaiian John Cummins, distinguished with his white hair and long white beard, Cecile Kainoa, her long black hair falling down her straight back and her fine features stoic. And Kimo Kainoa, all at once looking far more mature than his years. It was his seventeenth birthday, that day. Their father, Daniel, was conspicuous by his absence. He had died of a stroke while in jail.

Twenty-five ragged, hungry-looking Hawaiians were brought in, all in one batch. The crowd gasped at their pathetic appearance. In all, one hundred and ninety-one Royalists were on trial.

When Lot Lane was questioned, he said simply, as if to answer for all of them: *"I went to fight for my country and my Queen..."* *"We're not interested in that!"* snapped the prosecutor. Rat-faced and solemn, he brushed dandruff from the collar of his black suit, his long fingers flicking. *"We want to know where you got the guns!"* He raised his voice and fixed his eyes on Lot.

But Lot ignored the question and carried on making his own statements: *"You say I am a traitor! To whom? My country? My Queen? No! You are the traitors! To the people who gave you aloha in their own land. If I have done anything wrong against my country, then punish me. But I can only be punished if I have hurt my own land which God gave to us Hawaiians for life!"*

By now most of the crowd was on its feet, cheering. They were quickly quietened by the PG guards.

All the Royalists were found guilty. Their sentences ranged from one to five years hard labor. Some were fined a thousand dollars... others five thousand.

Many individuals had saved their own skins by deciding to give evidence against the Royalists. Samuel Nowlein and Henry Bertelmann were but two who were promised their lives in exchange for their testimony. They were delighted to be given their liberty. Bertelmann was particularly overcome. He wept for joy, then took sick and was unable to leave the Police Station for some time. Very little public attention was paid to him. But Nowlein aroused general contempt, threats and hatred. He'd formerly been such a close aide of the Queen.

Liliuokalani wrote:

"The knowledge of the secreting of arms on my premises, the distribution of munitions of war amongst the people who were guarding my house and grounds, has been imputed to me. Whether any arms were brought there, where they were, or what they were, I never took occasion to inquire. I never saw a single pistol or rifle by day or by night."

"I remember that I had occasion to scold my gardener for the disturbed condition in which I often found my plants. It seemed as though some persons had been digging up the ground, and re-

*placing the disturbed soil. But no arms were se-
creted by me or by my orders about the place from
the roof to the cellar, or from one end to the other
of the garden, nor were any kept there to my
knowledge, save parlor rifles and harmless old-
fashioned muskets..."*

While awaiting her own trial, Liliuokalani was
kept prisoner in the poorly furnished room in Iolani
Palace; the building which she had occupied as Queen
during the last days of its opulence.

Loyal Hawaiian friends and some foreign sym-
pathizers smuggled news in to her. It was always newspaper wrappings that covered the cakes, other food-
stuffs or flowers they brought her.

The monotonous beat of the armed guard's foot-
steps, back and forth, outside her door, irritated the
Queen's already frayed nerves.

On the fourth day of her imprisonment, her lawyer had informed her that she and six of the leaders of
the revolution were to be *"shot for treason."*

In her journal, the Queen wrote that her doctor
Donald McLelan had been in attendance on her for
three months prior to the revolt in January, 1895: *"As
I was suffering very severely from nervous prostra-
tion, he prescribed electricity. For two years I had
borne the long agony of suspense, a terrible strain,
which at last made great inroads on my strength."*
Further, in her memoranda dated April 18th, 1895:
*"7:45 a.m.... Dr. McLelan called... said might leave
off battery and only use when required... but to exercise often."*

And further:

"1:15 p.m.... Mr. Wilson called... gave him

my gold eye glasses to take to Lindsey and have him put in cleats to hold on the nose... also my gold pen to repair... Soup from Mrs. Sam Allen... cake from Mrs. Haalelea... bunches of pansies from Kaiaha Ward... bouquet of carnations from Miss Finckler... all sent to the Queen with much love. Was engaged for the rest of the day arranging my compositions..."

Liliuokalani worked on her now famous song, *"Aloha Oe,"* while imprisoned.

The following item appeared in the New York Evening Post on May 16, 1895:

"San Francisco, California, May 16,... Captain Julius A. Palmer Jr. who went to the Hawaiian Islands to investigate the state of affairs there, as special correspondent of the New York Evening Post, three months ago, arrived here on the Australia. He believes there will soon be a crisis there and that the end can only be the restoration of the monarchical form of government. He says there never will be harmony until the Monarchy is restored and Princess Kaiulani placed on the throne..."

Col. Ashford, ex-Attorney-General of Hawaii, who arrived on the same steamer, expressed similar views:

"There is a perfect reign of terror in the Islands; informers are everywhere. People do not dare speak in their own houses. There is everywhere a feeling of uncertainty, doubt and impending danger and ruin. Those who favored Annexation have made up their minds that it is impossible.

"The missionaries as we call most of the politi-

cal party in power, have claimed to be in favor of Annexation, but we have never been really. The Annexationists mistrust them now."

"As to the future. Well, Annexation is an impossibility and all are about agreed on that. Thurston has gone back, and it is publicly said that he is going to propose the restoration of a Monarchy with Kaiulani on the Throne..."

In September, 1895, the Independent commented:

"We quote from the Advertiser that: 'Mr. Thurston believed it would be better to do something than to sit still...' This expression is the very essence of Mr. Thurston's character. There is an ever increasing number of people in these islands who think it unfortunate that Mr. Thurston could not sit still in January, 1893..."

In an article published by the Independent, September 1895, the poet Joaquin Miller referred to: *"... the feast of fat things taken from the confiding Queen of Hawaii and her simple people...* He continued: *"The Queen's land alone... which they seized... had brought her the best half of a quarter of a million. The Honolulu Water Works, perfected under the late King, and being the property of the Crown, brings $100,000 clear profit. The Custom House is a mine of gold..."*

On the Republic of Hawaii Government, Miller wrote further:

"...Reverting again to the little family oligarchy which has been masquerading under the name of a Republic, it is safe to say that because of its misrepresentations and money-getting propensities, it is almost as odious abroad as it is at home,

where the grass is beginning to grow in the street because of stagnation. And that is why London and Berlin are hinting to Washington that if we don't want the Islands, the present government should be quietly laid aside, as a misfit shoe, and the little Princess (Kaiulani) placed at the head, in case the Queen still refuses to make further claim to her once prosperous and happy Hawaii..."

Now it could be clearly seen by many: The heir apparent was being purposely kept away from Hawaii for political reasons. Despite her terrible anguish over the bad news from home, somehow her life went on.

In the late 1890's, during one of their visits to the South of France, Kaiulani and her father befriended a young man, Nevinson William de Courcy (nicknamed Toby).

The son of an English Baron, Toby was a qualified architect and civil engineer and was regarded as an eligible bachelor and ideal escort for well-bred young ladies in those Victorian days.

A long correspondence continued between Kaiulani and Toby, who was six years her senior. She referred to him as her *"Father Confessor"* and in her letters was warm and confiding:

Sunday

My dear Toby,

Very many thanks for yours of the 28th. I also heard from Sib that she had seen you - You both say the other was looking very pale and thin, Mon Ami qu est ce qu'il-y-a? Surely you are not ailing! And I trust above all things you are not suffering from mal au coeur. I have been very seedy. Papa was over in town so he consulted the Dr. I have been suffering from too much worry!!! So I am to sleep a great deal etc. Evidently dancing is not harmful otherwise Papa would have prevented my going to a dance on Wednesday. Toby I feel so naughty, I have such a nice flirtation on pour le moment. Don't be shocked, and leave your lecture until we meet in Menton - It is too good to believe that I shall have the pleasure of seeing you soon - won't we talk! I have such piles to tell you. I have Gertie Somers staying with me and also a Miss Brander - we are about the three biggest flirts you could find, so we simply have a lovely time. Just fancy Pa went to London on Tuesday last and returned yesterday. We had quite a nice time by ourselves!!!

It is decided we start on the 30th and reach Menton Jan 1 rather a ghastly day to reach a place. I had a letter from Lilian Kennedy. She seems to be having a perfectly A.I. time - fancy - they went to a luncheon, she and her Ma - and 7 men were invited to meet them. There weren't any women in the place. Do you think you'd like to live there?

I am quite shocked to think that you should long for "Absinthe". We intend going to the Louvre again - You see Fat George is the attraction. Madam van Asbeck is there again. Do you know her? She was chiefly conspicuous by the absence - I should like to see that charade. I think it must be rather fine! I did not know you could do that sort of thing!

An excited, scribbled note followed, asking Toby to bring all the men he knew to a forthcoming dance.

La Chaire
Rozel Jersey

My Dear Toby

I am really ashamed of myself for having delayed so long in acknowledging your letter. I thank you very much for your kind wishes on my birthday - I laughed very much when I thought of my other birthday - what fun we had that night!

At last we have got back to our little Jersey home. I was quite glad to get back though the trees are all bare, and the weather far from nice - still, it is the one place that I can boss the show, so to speak. I am feeling very dull indeed. Papa has a bad cold, and is consequently in the vilest of tempers. It is most unfortunate as he has been free from colds for so long. He has an idea that he is going to pip which is most annoying - however one must put up with these little annoyances.

We spent a week in town, and then stayed a week with some friends at Southsea. I saw the "Prisoner of Zenda" and "A Night Out" whilst in town - I simply howled with laughter at the latter - it was really too funny - especially when the old Papa comes rushing in with a huge red chest protector on. I really thought I was going to have a fit. If you are up in town and want to laugh - just go there. We were pretty gay at the Langham - had a charming suite of rooms, and simply went the pace while we were up.

We are going down to Menton about the 19th of December - George O'Dell is there already - I am looking forward to seeing you, my Father Confessor - I hope we may have a pleasant winter. I think Mrs. Suggett will join us - without Jean Erls - your particular friend. I am very fond of Mrs. Suggett - "if you want me - I'm just here!, her particular phrase...

One of my young men came to see me yesterday - I am supposed to be polishing him off - I can't make up my mind to do so just yet must have a little more fun as my fling is limited - I intend to get as much amusement this winter as I possibly can, There is a possibility of my being married in April to a man I don't care much for either way - rather a gloomy outlook - but "noblesse oblige" - I must have been born under an unlucky star - as I seem to have my life planned out for me in such a way that I cannot alter it. Do you blame me if I have my fling now - better now than afterwards.

My engagement is a "great secret" - approved of by Mr. Davies and my Father - it is being kept secret for political reasons. Personally I think it wrong like this, as it is unfair to the men I meet now - especially if they take any interest in me.

I am not feeling at all fit, as I had two teeth taken out on my birthday. My jaw was fearfully cut up trying to remove the bits as they splintered. I have had a very bad time of it, as you may fancy. I hope I shall soon get one of your cheery letters, that is if you have nothing else to do.

With love from Papa and myself
Believe me
Yours ever sincerely,
KAIULANI OF HAWAII
Saturday.

More to Toby from Ravensdale, the Davies' new house at Tunbridge Wells, written July 4th, 1897:

I have not left for Scotland as you will see by the direction, instead I am wending my way Jerseywards. I start on Monday with Elise, and Papa will join us in a week or ten days. He intends going down to Bournemouth to see the Bishop of Honolulu, and also…? The fact of the matter is, he intends taking a little jaunt around the country and enjoying himself.

I shall find it very dull in Jersey as my particular "amusement" is in Woolwich for the summer.. Is it not provoking? It is just my luck when I am dull not to have anything on hand.

I have lived on milk for the past two months, and am not taking very much exercise. Consequently I am growing fairly fat. I think I can stand a little more flesh on my bones, still I don't want to grow fat, it is so vulgar you know. Another reason I am growing stout, I have not been able to be up to any of my larks. I've quite got out of the way of flirting! I don't believe I could do it to save my skin. Now, don't laugh!

I am really feeling very much better, but have still to be very careful. I was so annoyed a few days back. I managed to get down for breakfast and stayed up fairly late in the evening, having also played croquet during the afternoon, when on my way to bed, I again had one of my fainting fits. It showed me that I must be more careful, but all the same it is very hard lines, and I hate posing as an invalid.

Where are you going to spend your summer? There is some talk of my going over to pay my revered Aunt a visit, but as yet things are extremely undecided. They talk of Annexation, but whether they will get it is quite another thing. However, things are in a very bad way out there, and I am now pretty certain that we shall never have back our own again... I am really rather sorry the way the whole thing has finished up, much better have a republic than to lose our nationality altogether... I am very sorry for my people, as they will hate being taken over by another nation.

If I went over to see my Aunt I would only stay about three weeks there and return again here. My ex-Guardian is going out to Hawaii the latter part of September. He has a great deal of interest in sugar, and he seems anxious about it. He may think it advisable for me to return home the end of this winter.

The friendship between Princess Kaiulani and Toby de Courcy continued through the years of 1895, '96, and '97, when they both holidayed in Menton, in the South of France.

He kept her letters for the rest of his life.

As for Kaiulani's secret engagement, it was popularly thought that she would someday marry Prince David Kawananakoa, who was a nephew of Queen Kapiolani's and a lineal descendant of King Kaumualii of Kauai. It was as though the engagement had been hurriedly arranged in a desperate attempt to strengthen the badly beleaguered Throne.

Whatever the intent and whoever the betrothed, somewhere along the line of troubled events the plan seems to have been abandoned as no engagement was ever publicly announced.

⋆⋆⋆⋆⋆⋆⋆

he trial of Queen Liliuokalani opened on February 8, 1895. She was charged with *"misprision of treason."*

Entering the Throne Room wearing a simple black dress and hat and carrying a lauhala fan, the Queen was calm and dignified as she faced the men whom she once welcomed in the same room when she was reigning queen. In a firm voice, she said: *"I owe no allegiance to the Provisional Government established by a small minority of the foreign population... nor to any power or anyone, save the will of my people and the welfare of my country..."*

Another part of her statement was read to the court: *"To prevent the shedding of the blood of my people, native and foreign alike, I quietly yielded to the armed forces brought against my throne... and submitted to the government of the United States, the decision of my rights and those of the Hawaiian people..."*

Liliuokalani's trial lasted four days. She was then isolated again in her rooms at the palace for another twenty days... then summoned to hear the verdict: *"Five years imprisonment at hard labor... and a $5000 fine."*

After eight months, the Queen was released and given a *"confidential pardon"* by President Dole of the Provisional Government.

Most of the imprisoned 191 Royalists were also released or had their sentences greatly reduced, following waves of protest from all over the United States.

After leaving her *"prison"* at Iolani Palace, Liliuokalani was allowed to return to her residence at Washington Place. Placed under constant surveillance by PG guards, however, she could only leave the house with their permission.

In January, 1896, the Queen was released from parole, but forbidden to leave the Island of Oahu. She moved to her ocean retreat at Waikiki where her friends, who had been too fearful to visit Washington Place, now felt free to join her; to weep, to sing and to talk freely, at last, about the tragic events of the last three years.

Still in her mind was the plan to visit the United States to present her case to the American people. She was awaiting the day when she'd be free to travel...

"Hawaii for the Hawaiians" was now just a faint cry...

In December, the Queen informed President Dole of the Republic, that she wished to travel again to the mainland; mainly to San Francisco and Oakland, to visit friends and relatives of her late husband.

Cautioning her against traveling in the harsh cold of winter. Dole was really concerned that she might visit Washington; to stir up trouble again.

Still, he graciously granted passports to *"Liliuokalani of Hawaii"* and her traveling companions. Sensing the undertones, the Queen wrote in her journal *"...every word, every look, every act of mine, was being noted down by spies, to be reported somewhere to my hurt."*

Kaiulani wrote to her aunt:

> *37 Avenue Marceau,*
> *Paris*
> *May 9th, 1897.*

My Dear Aunt,

> *Very many thanks for your kind letter.*
>
> *Annie's sudden death has been a very great shock to both of us - I can hardly realize that the dear girl has gone. (Kaiulani's half-sister, Annie Cleghorn)*
>
> *I am sorry to say that I am not feeling at all well.*
>
> *My nerves are all out of order and I suffer continually from headaches.*
>
> *I daresay you have already heard of the awful catastrophe which took place here at Bazar de Charite. I have never heard of anything so fearful in my life. Nearly all of the 117 victims were women and young ones too. There is a count next*

door who has lost his two daughters, girls of 18 and 19.

What strikes one so is it's being in one's own station of life, the smartest society women of Paris.

The death of the Duchesse d'Alemon throws the Austrian, Belgian and Bavarian Courts into mourning, not counting the Arleans and King of Naples families. Just imagine all those people gone in less than half an hour. And the dreadful agony they must have suffered. I have never seen any place so overcast as the gay City of Paris - you see all the people selling, were connected with the highest aristocracy of France.

I hope that you are keeping well and that you are enjoying yourself in Washington. I am going on the 19ᵗʰ to Ravensdale, Tunbridge Wells to stay with the Davies. I hope the change will do me some good.

Meanwhile, eager Annexationists in Honolulu were heartened as Grover Cleveland was ousted in the November 1896 elections and Republican William McKinley became President. He wasted no time in submitting the Hawaiian Annexation Treaty to the Senate in June of 1897.

President McKinley's choice of a U.S. Minister to Hawaii, was Harold M. Sewall, an ardent advocate of Hawaiian annexation. In a letter to the Daily Press in Maine, dated June 28ᵗʰ 1894, he had savagely attacked President Cleveland's Hawaiian policy.

Word of this event reached Kaiulani and her father on the Island of Jersey where they were holidaying at their favorite retreat. Kaiulani was despondent over the news as it now seemed that Hawaii would be annexed to America.

Archie Cleghorn and his daughter discussed the situation far into the night. Kaiulani felt that her *"exile"* was now senseless and that she was no longer able to endure her absence from home. Whatever Hawaii's fate might be, she wanted to be there to share it with her people. Her life had no real meaning in Europe.

The next morning they made plans for her return to the islands.

Throughout June 1897, Kaiulani still holidayed for the summer, with her father. They enjoyed the long, balmy days in a small cottage nestled in a copse of trees, on the Island of Jersey. The setting always reminded Kaiulani of home.

One afternoon, their peace was spoiled, when news reached them that Annexation was imminent in Hawaii. *"After all the long struggles of the Royalists, it's come to this…"* Cleghorn reflected.

They made arrangements to sail from Southampton on October 9. On their way to Hawaii, Kaiulani and her father visited Washington. They called on the deposed Queen, who now spent as much time as possible in the capital. Her mission was to explore any means of righting the wrong done to the Hawaiian Kingdom.

While busily preparing for the trip home at long last, Kaiulani wrote to her father from Scotland:

Johnston Lodge,
Austruther,
Fife.
August, 1897.

My dearest Papa,

I wrote to Liverpool on Saturday for ten pounds, as I was out of money. I am going to stay four days with the Barbours on Tuesday 24th... their address is Baledmund, Pitlochry.

I shall return here on the 28th. The Somers have asked me to stay with them on my way south, and the Wodehouses want us also, So my idea is to leave here on the 7th and stay with the Somers until the 10th. I thought you might go to the Ws on the 10th until the 14th.

The Davies want us on the 17th until the 20th, the two days we might spend in town.

Lady Wiseman wants me from the 24th for a few days. Perhaps you might go from St. Leonards to stay a few days at Bournemouth and also Brighton, while I go and stay with Lady Wiseman.

I want to stay a couple of days in town to pack my boxes. Have you got the address of the Hotel the Watsons spoke to you about.

May wrote and said she thought twenty four pounds too little - considering we are paying her passage out and back again, I think it extremely nasty.

I am going to write her a sharp letter, because if I have to look out for anyone I must be doing so now.

I hope you had a pleasant journey, I expect a letter from you in the morning. We have had fairly

fine days since I came but Scotch weather is pro-
verbially bad.

I am feeling very fit and hope I shall be
alright. Have you seen anything of Mrs. Stewart?
Please give her my love.

Mr. Davies has sent me a plan of the ship,
and also the number of my room. I wonder if I
shall be alone.

With aloha from all and heaps of love.

From your loving,
VIKE.
Sunday night.

Another letter from Scotland quickly followed:

August 19, 1897

My dearest Papa, You never seem happy un-
less you are imagining your letters have gone
astray - of course I have received all your letters.
I don't mention every one or all the dates.

I have already written to Mary and told her
that we would pay her fare out and back again.
My account is she has not half finished doing up
my old things. You must not grumble at the ac-
count as I am trying to get all my things, so that I
won't need to buy any out there. Besides there
are heaps of things that have to be bought for the
house such as tea cloths and mats and all sorts of
small things. Then there are all the presents. You
know quite well that all the children will expect
something; besides Mrs. Sproull said I ought to
take out a large stock of ribbons, gloves, hand-
kerchiefs and those sorts of things... you seem to
forget that I may not return for some time.

If we were together now we would probably have a violent quarrel over this, but I am sure you will understand when things are put to you mildly.

You seem surprised at my having any enjoyment at all.. I had an offer of the box for the "Geisha" and thought I might take the opportunity to see it. The next might we were invited to see the "Midsummer Night's Dream". I am sure that had you had the invitation you would have gone,

I have sent the list of the linen to Mr. Davies, it will be sent overland. Well I hope you will enjoy yourself.

> With love from us all.
> Your loving child,
> *KAIULANI*

As planned, with all the last minute errands and farewells completed, on October 9, 1897, Kaiulani sailed from Southampton to New York on the first leg of her journey home.

It was seven days before her twenty-second birthday.

On her way home in San Francisco, the young Princess was once again inundated by reporters.. Impressed by her beauty and her manner, they discredited cruel rumors that were being widely circulated about her by the Provisional Government.

A reporter from the Examiner wrote:

A Barbarian Princess? Not a bit of it. Not even a hemi-semi-demi Barbarian. Rather the very flower - an exotic - of civilization. The Princess Kaiulani is charming, fascinating, individual. She has the taste and style of a French woman; the admirable repose and soft voice of an English woman. She was gowned for dinner in a soft, black, high necked frock, with the latest Parisian touches in every fold; a bunch of pink roses in her belt and a slender gold chain around her neck, dangling a lorgnette. She is tall, of willowy slenderness, erect and graceful, with a small, pale face, full red lips, soft expression, dark eyes, a very good nose, and a cloud of crimpy black hair knotted high.

The writer from The Call had nothing but praise for her also:

She is beautiful. There is no portrait that does justice to her expressive, small, proud face. She is exquisitely slender and graceful, holds herself like a Princess, like a Hawaiian - and I know of no simile more descriptive of grace and dignity than this last.

Her accent says London; her figure says New York; her heart says Hawaii. But she is more than a beautiful pretender to an abdicated throne; she has been made a woman of the world by the life she has led.

When Kaiulani and her father, an route to Honolulu, made their special trip to Washington to see Liliuokalani, they found her longing to return to the Islands. She suffered terribly from the extreme climate of the Capital City and was greatly disheartened by McKinley's action in reviving the Annexation Bill. She hoped that, by conducting her cause with dignity and persistence, justice would eventually be done and her throne restored. If that failed, she would still have to fight for the Crown Lands, which were the traditional inheritance of the Monarchy in Hawaii and the source of almost all of her and Kaiulani's income.

It was the first time that she and Kaiulani had met in eight years and the Queen was very reluctant to let them go. Shortly after leaving, they received the following letter from her:

> *October 26, 1897*
> *The Ebbett House*
> *Washington, D.C.*

> *My dear Niece,*
>
> *Your short visit to me has been very pleasant, and we have not ceased to talk of you. I wish you could have stayed a month or two longer at least until the question of the Annexation was settled. I think your presence here would have done some good, but as I knew that you and your father were both anxious to get home I naturally kept quiet.*
>
> *Another reason was I had not the means to detain you which is another and most important point. during your stay I was glad to know that your heart and that of your father lay in the right direction that is: you are interested in the course of your people.*

For the second time Liliuokalani writes that she has heard that Kaiulani is to be offered the Throne of Hawaii.

> *Here is an opportunity for me to let you know something which I feel you ought to know - and I leave it for your own good judgment to guide you in your decision. It has been made known to me that it is the intention of the members of the Republican Government of Hawaii to ask you to take*

the Throne of Hawaii in case they failed in their scheme of Annexation. That you should have nothing to say about the managing - that shall be theirs still, but you are to be a figurehead only. If you were to accept their proposition there would be no change whatever in the situation of the country for the good of the people or for all classes of men or for business advancements. You would only be in Mr. Dole's place, despised, and as he is now, in fear of his life.

You will have a few followers who will love you, but it will only be the 2600 who now are supporting Dole's Government and still have over 80,000 opposing you. It is through their mismanagement that their Government has not been a success. It is for this reason that knowing their instability they want to annex Hawaii to America. Another reason why their Government has not been a success is the people are not with them and they are fully aware of the fact. So as a last trial they wish you to take it. I have shown you in the above, the danger. Now let me explain to you another phase. If you decline to accept the position of Queen which will place you more in favor with the people, the Republic of Hawaii will fall through as even now they can barely maintain themselves, then there will be a call from the people for a "plebiscite", then I say "accept it", for it is maintained by the love of the people.

I think Mr. T.H. Davies and George MacFarlane are knowing of this plan and I know approve of it. George said to me when I was in San Francisco that you and I ought to agree on *this matter, that I ought to yield to you as the R. of Hawaii, never to consent to have me reign again, that it were better if we agreed on you. I did not give him any answer because I had no right to. The people's wish is paramount with me, and what they say I abide by, Now my dear Child, for you are very dear to me, I hope you will act wisely for your own sake and be cautious in signing any documents they may present to you, reading over thoroughly and understanding it before hand - for they are the greatest liars, and deceitful in all their undertakings and your young heart is too pure to see their wickedness. I mean the PGs. My Dear Niece, may the Almighty help you. Love to your father and I think it well you should show him this letter.*

With lots of Love,
Your affectionate Aunt,
LILIUOKALANI.

Mr. Davies wrote a curt letter to the Queen in November, 1897...

"I take the liberty of saying that neither Mr. Damon or Mr. Macfarlane or anyone else has ever conferred with me in regard to putting forward claims on behalf of Princess Kaiulani to the Throne of Hawaii. I am also certain that under no circumstances would the Princess Kaiulani have accepted the Throne except with the approval of Your Majesty and at the joint request of Hawaiians and foreigners.

He refers to the rumor as a *"melancholy incident"* at a time when those *"in faithful service to Hawaii should stick together"*.

At last, Kaiulani eyes brightened at the sight of the majestic mountains rising behind Honolulu. The growing town below had spread over a much wider area in the eight years of her absence. She didn't know whether she was pleased with the development or not. For now, it was enough just to drink in the sight of this jewel in the middle of the vast Pacific; her home.

A light shower of rain blessed the arrival of the S.S. *Australia* as the big ship edged into the crusty side of Oceanic Wharf. It was November 9, 1897. Kaiulani left here a child, now she was a woman.

A huge, excited crowd made a colorful mosaic on the wharf. People had flocked from all parts of the Islands to welcome their beloved Princess home. She was their *"last hope."*

Many were openly clinging to each other and weeping, venting long pent-up sorrows. Others were beaming and carrying strings of ilima, pikake and maile leis on their arms; gifts for Kaiulani, their returning alii. She represented more to them than they could ever explain. Her beauty inspired them; her mana kindled old flames within their breasts.

The Princess received friends on board the ship for half an hour. Eva Parker, Prince David and a handful of others crowded into the small cabin. Kaiulani scanned the crowd from the deck. Finally, she left the ship and drove with her party, in a landau, directly to the Royal Mausoleum in Nuuanu. Kaiulani had nursed a long yearning to visit her mother's resting place. She touched the cold marble fronting the tomb with the inscription: *"Princess Miriam Likelike, 1851-1887."*

"I'm home Mama," she said softly. *"I'm home."*

Stepping onto the precious soil of Ainahau and surrounded by familiar faces full of love and welcome, Kaiulani revelled in being home again. After getting settled, one of the first things she did was seek out Fairy, the faithful white saddle pony of her childhood, who was now eighteen years old. There in the corner of a field Fairy still waited for her. Kaiulani hugged and patted him and then gently mounted the old horse. The ride was not as vigorous as it had been 8 years before, but nothing ever felt so good as the cool breezes from Manoa caressing her face while old Fairy snorted into a canter.

The next day, Hawaiians, by the hundred, formed a colorful procession up the long, palm-lined driveway to the Princess' residence at Waikiki. All carried leis, fruit and other gifts, some alive and kicking, for their beloved Kaiulani. It was a comfort just to know she was back home with them at last. They had all been through many a dark night of anguish. In her delicate frame rested the last glimpse of their monarchy.

Kaiulani received them warmly, for ten hours. Many familiar faces, aging now, brought up long buried memories. At nine o'clock that night, exhausted, she had to retire, emotionally drained by it all.

Just after her arrival home, Kaiulani's first letter to her Aunt Liliuokalani read:

> *Ainahau,*
> *Waikiki,*
> *H.Is.,*
> *November 17, 1897,*

My Dear Aunt,

I must just send you a few lines to let you know of our safe arrival. Since we got here, we have been so busy, what with receiving and getting the house in order, I am fairly worn out.

Last Saturday the Hawaiians came out to see me. There were several hundred, and by six o'clock I didn't know what to do with myself, I was so tired. It made me so sad to see so many of the Hawaiians looking so poor - in the old days I am sure there were not so many people almost destitute.

Before I say anything I want to thank you for letting me use your span. They are splendid horses, and will soon be in very good condition. It is awfully kind of you to lend them to me, and I will take good care of them.

I find the place very much changed. I refer to Ainahau. The trees have grown out of all recognition; it is really a very beautiful house and very cool.

A great many of the haoles have called but I am at home for the first time tomorrow. I dread it as I am so very nervous. I have asked Mrs. Carter to help me receive, It is so kind of her to come all this way out - She and her husband came all the way out the day I arrived.

I eat poi and raw fish as though I had never left, and I find I have not forgotten my Hawaiian.

Well, Auntie Dear, I must close. I will write again very soon, but at present I feel the heat so much, I can't settle to anything.

Goodbye, with much love,
I remain
Ever your affectionate niece,
KAIULANI.

When, on Nov. 20th, a new delegation of native Hawaiians left for the U.S. to fight annexation, Minister Sewall became quite disturbed by all this *"Royalist activity"*. He was also apprehensive of the rumored coup to place Princess Kaiulani on the throne, as he had personally witnessed the great outpouring of affection for her when she returned home.

The pro-Annexation newspaper; The Advertiser stated in articles that it was not afraid of anything Kaiulani might do, as the Monarchy was *"such a thing of the past..."* However, it didn't mind calling her *"Princess"*, as long as she didn't cause any trouble.

She wrote again to her Aunt, who was still in Washington, on January 5th, 1898...

Thank God Annexation is not a fact. the people here are not half so happy as when I first came back - I find everything so much changed, and more especially among the rising generation of Hawaiians and half whites. I think it is a great pity as they are trying to ape the foreigners and they do not succeed.

In 1898, other letters from Ainahau to her aunt in Washington followed:

Papa and I are going up to stay with the Parkers. We leave on the 23rd of June, and I fancy I will stay there until the hot weather passes and I want to go away before the 4th of July festivities come off. I am sure you would be disgusted if you could see the way the town is decorated for the American troops. Honolulu is making a fool of itself, and I only hope we won't all be ridiculed.

(The 4th of July festivities to which Kaiulani bitterly refers, celebrated not only American Independence Day for the Americans living in Hawaii, but also the fourth anniversary of the founding of the Republic of Hawaii.)

A family friend wrote that *"Kaiulani hid the bitterness in her heart from the public, and strove to do what was expected of her."* After the Princess' arrival back in Honolulu from England, she became one of the two vice-presidents of the newly formed Red Cross Society and also quickly involved herself in the work of the Hawaiian Relief Society and other social and charitable enterprises.

To her aunt she wrote:

I should have written sooner, but writing is such a tax to my head here. I wonder why that is. I don't feel the least bit settled. I suppose it is because the old natives are all dead or married.

I am suffering from the heat, but that is to be expected, but I also have hay fever very badly which is extremely disagreeable, though it is harmless.

Her aunt's previous letter had referred to *"possible overtures"* of those in power, but Kaiulani replied that she was mistaken:

The people of the Government are not particularly nice to me, excepting Mrs. Damon and Mrs. Dole. I think they are very sorry to see me here, especially as I give them no cause to complain.

I am sure you will be very sorry to hear of the death of Mrs. Wilson (she was lady-in-waiting to Liliuokalani when she was Queen, and was her only companion during her imprisonment). *I was very shocked, as I did not even know she was ill. Poor woman, she was always such a good friend of the Aliis. Such a number of our friends have died during the past few years.*

After Kaiulani's return to Hawaii, there was much speculation regarding her choice of a husband. During 1898, she was romantically linked with two dashing young *haoles*. One, the broad-shouldered Captain Putnam Bradley Strong, arrived in the islands on the troopship, Peru. He was a daily visitor to Ainahau and he and Kaiulani went horseback riding and swimming in the Waikiki surf until his ship sailed for Manila.

The second romance involved Andrew Adams, a handsome young New Englander who wrote for the *Advertiser.* Archie Cleghorn liked him so much that he invited him to stay at Ainahau, then found him a job as overseer on a plantation. Adams and Kaiulani were greatly attracted to one another, but they quarreled frequently and eventually became friends and nothing more.

Most of her close friends felt that the Princess was preoccupied with too many worries to be seriously concerned with romance and, although there were many in love with her both here and abroad, she gave her heart to no man.

On February 19, 1898, Kaiulani gave a luau at Ainahau to celebrate the thirtieth birthday of David Kawananakoa, her *"cousin"*, who was seven years her senior. About a hundred guests, mostly Hawaiian, attended and the singing was lusty and long, almost drowning out the sounds of the Hawaiian National Band that played valiantly beneath the banyan tree.

> HO'OPAU: *(To finish)*
> *And the Hawaiians cried for the past...*
> *For the grass houses of their kuleanas disappeared*
>   *and returned to the earth*
> *which first gave them life*
> *And they looked for the tall coconut palms of their*
>   *grandfathers' youth...*
> *The sentinels of the Islands...*
> *Were they to disappear too?*

After a lengthy stay in Washington, where she wearily continued the struggle to regain her throne, Queen Liliuokalani returned to Honolulu aboard the *Gaelic* on August 1, 1898. A huge crowd of Hawaiians waited on the wharf. Very few haoles were present. The Queen appeared at the head of the gangplank, dressed entirely in black. Her people greeted her with silence. She gazed down at the sea of upturned faces and at last called, *"Aloha!"* to them. The crowd then cried *"Aloha!"* in response.

Men, women and children wept, as she crossed the wharf, stately and dignified on the arm of Prince David Kawananakoa. In the moonlight, Princess Kaiulani emerged from the crowd to greet her aunt. They drove to Washington Place where the driveway was ablaze with torches; symbol of their family.

Two aged Hawaiian chamberlains wearing black broadcloth suits and tall silk hats stood on either side of the gateway. Kukui nuts bound in ti leaves formed the flaming torches they held. The oily lamps gave off a soft vapor. With their old backs straight, the torch-bearers stood there all night, proudly guarding their Queen's residence. They had performed the same service for her, during better days at the palace.

An abundance of green maile leaves encircled the white pillars and door frames. One word was written over the door in red lettering: *"Pumehana"*, meaning *"warmest greetings."*

Inside, the Queen sat at her own table, in her own home, again, An island meal of raw fish and poi and fruit was served to her and her guests, while young girls gently waved white feather kahilis over her head.

In the grounds, the chanting went on for hours; greeting and praising the returning monarch. Later, all her old retainers came to greet her. Their white heads bowed before her as they fell to their knees. The Queen called each of them by name and wiped tears from her eyes.

he Annexationists got their way at last.

Annexation Day, long dreaded by the Hawaiians, dawned on August 12, 1898. The ceremony was to take place in spite of the protests of both Hawaii's hereditary rulers and most of its populace.

With the Republic of Hawaii now four years old. President McKinley in Washington set the date for transference of sovereignty to the United States.

Sanford Ballard Dole, the President of the Republic, and Harold M. Sewall, U.S. Minister to Hawaii, busied themselves with plans for a ceremony to hoist *"Old Glory"* atop Iolani Palace.

The largest American flag the Navy could find was raised precisely at noon on the central tower of Iolani Palace. A U.S. Naval Band lustily played *"Star Spangled Banner"*, while two smaller U.S. flags were jerkily hoisted on each of the corner towers of the palace.

Within six minutes, the Hawaiian Islands had become a part of the United States and Annexation was at last a fact. The joy that was expected at the scene was strangely absent. Many reported seeing the wives of American officials dabbing at their eyes with handkerchiefs. Even the faces of Sanford Dole and some members of his Cabinet had turned pale during the ceremony, which was mercifully brief. Spectators were seen hurrying away to waiting carriages, apparently with no desire to linger at the scene. It was too sad a time, bitter and heartbreaking for too many.

Frequent showers of rain swept over the crowd.

Hawaii was a nation no more. The burning torch went out forever.

One writer from San Francisco, Mabel Craft observed: *"In front of the Executive Building there were Americans, Japanese, Chinese... but no Hawaiians. The ceremonies had the tension of an execution."*

And many other vivid descriptions were published:

"When the last strains of Hawaii Ponoi trembled out of hearing, the wind suddenly held itself back and as the Hawaiian flag left the track, it dropped and folded and descended lifelessly to Earth. The day was cloudy and there were light showers."

One satirical report said:

"Rumor spread telling there would be trap doors (on the speakers stand) and as the Hawaiian banner lowered, President Dole and his Cabinet would sink slowly from sight, amidst a lurid display of colored lights and smoke."

And after the ceremony, a newsman wrote:

"We have slept our last sleep as Hawaiians. Tomorrow we arise as residents of an American territory. We must accept the situation and make the most of it, for it is an irrevocable one no matter what some folks say." He then called on the United States asking: *"Uncle Sam shake! It's your turn to stand treat. The call's on you!"*

Another recalled:

"Hawaii Ponoi was being played as the Hawaiian flag was lowered for the last time. Before it ended, the native musicians threw down their instruments and ran away, around the corner of the Palace... to weep in private."

Editor Edmund Norrie of the Independent wrote: *"Farewell dear flag, farewell dear emblem of love and hospitality... of a trusting, confiding and childlike people with hearts that know no guile."*

The Queen and Princess Kaiulani had received invitations to attend the Annexation ceremony, but they politely declined. Instead, they spent the day surrounded by loyal friends and Royalists at the Queen's private residence; Washington place on Beretania St.

Having lost the throne irretrievably, Liliuokalani, with vastly diminished hope, left once again in November, 1898, for an indefinite stay in Washington where her fight would now be to regain the Crown Lands. The confiscation of these lands by the new Government was a severe blow to the Queen as most of her income was derived from these hereditary holdings.

Kaiulani was very upset at her aunt's departure and, as the *SS Coptic* sailed away with the ex-Queen on board, she fell into a depression. Neither she nor the Queen knew they had embraced for the last time.

Colonel MacFarlane, the Queen's confidential advisor and representative, tried to comfort Kaiulani and lift her spirits by pointing out that the American government respected both their positions and would surely provide an income for the Queen and herself and that she would remain a leader of her people in Hawaii.

Kaiulani quietly replied: *"Yes, but I shan't be much of a real Princess shall I? they haven't left me much to live for. I don't talk about it... I try not to grieve my father who watches over me so devotedly and seeks to make up to me for all the love I have lost. For his sake, I try not to mind... to appear bright and happy... but I think my heart is broken."*

Colonel MacFarlane added that, when on January 30th, 1893, Kaiulani received the cables that broke the news of the Monarchy's overthrow, her heart suffered a shock from which she never fully recovered.

His statement seemed to be borne out by her letters from abroad to friends and relatives in which she often referred to her *"good health"* or *"good spirits."* But, in the years following the arrival of those three shattering telegrams, she constantly referred to never-ending ailments such as La Grippe (influenza), headaches, nervousness, hay fever and a lack of energy. To her aunt she wrote that she suffered continually from headaches and during her last year abroad, she refused countless invitations because of *"indisposition."*

From Ainahau, she wrote to her aunt who was once again installed in Washington. The bitterness she felt at the situation in Hawaii since the American take-over was apparent in her letter:

...Daily, we as a great race are being subjected to a great deal of misery, and the more I see of the American soldiers about town, the more I am unable to tolerate them, what they stand for and the way we are belittled, it is enough to ruin one's faith in God...'

Last week some Americans came to the house and knocked rather violently at the door, and when they had stated their cause they wished to know if it would be permissible for the Ex-Princess to have her picture taken with them. Oh, will they never

leave us alone? They have now taken away ev-
erything from us and it seems there is left but little,
and that little our very life itself. We live now in
such a semi-retired way, that people wonder if
we even exist any more. I too wonder, and to what
purpose?

Reluctant to relinquish control, the same faction
that overthrew the Monarchy continued to govern the
islands for almost two years longer.

Later, Lorrin Thurston openly admitted that there
had been a plan by members of the *"committee"* to
overthrow the Monarchy completely from the time
Liliuokalani ascended the throne.

More and more, Kaiulani looked for excuses to
get away from Honolulu, finding conditions there
unbearable under the new regime.

Eva Parker's forthcoming wedding at the Parker
Ranch, on the island of Hawaii provided Kaiulani with
another opportunity to leave Honolulu. On the 7th of
December. 1898. Kaiulani and a group of friends
sailed on the steamer *Kinau*.

The Parker Ranch, occupying most of the cool,
elevated mountain region of Waimea, was known for
its grand way of life and was the center of the Big
Island's most important social events.

From the tone of her latest letter to her father,
Kaiulani enjoyed attending Eva Parker's enormous
wedding at Mana (the seat of the Parker Ranch) and
the many holiday festivities that followed.

In the first week of the New Year, 1899, guests
began to leave the ranch and return to their respective
islands. But, Kaiulani was reluctant to return to Honolulu and stayed on at Mana with other wedding

guests that tarried.

Kaiulani often rode off alone on one of the many trails at the ranch. She wanted to be alone with her thoughts, but they would always torment her so that she raced back at full gallop to rejoin her friends. Memories of her life in England brought pangs; she could still hear the clipped voices of her friends; their merry laughter. It now seemed like another lifetime… During one of her lone rides, she suddenly noticed a strange eerie silence had descended; there was no wind, no sound from the nearby stream; even the birds had stopped chirping. The silence thundered. Then, from out of nowhere an old Hawaiian man appeared on the trail in front of her. Her horse shied and she was almost thrown from the saddle. She felt annoyance growing inside her, as she settled her mount down. How dare anyone jump out and startle her! The old man's eyes caught her as she faced him. They were unusually bright and youthful, she thought, in such an old face. His hair was thick and white; his skin dark brown and lined with age. He was dressed simply in a clean, white long-sleeved shirt and black pants and a red bandana was knotted about his neck. His feet were bare.

At first she thought he must be just one of *"the locals"* who would soon prostrate himself in front of her and begin to recite endless prayers or greetings. Many times since she returned, she had been greeted in this way, because she was an alii.

"Please," she thought. *"Not now! I don't have time for any of this!"*

She spurred her horse, but the animal would not move. Then the old man's voice rang out as he addressed her in Hawaiian.

All her Hawaiian blood surged inside her and she knew in that instant that he was a kahuna.

"Beware young alii!" he said, *"Rain clouds gather overhead!"* His words were very colorful; full of symbolism and imagery and she realized that she was suddenly as fluent again in her understanding of the Hawaiian language, as she was in her childhood.

He intoned on with mention of her dead mother; that the same clouds that engulfed Likelike, now threatened her daughter.

He spoke of family secrets too dark to even comprehend and Kaiulani felt as if she would faint.

His voice was trailing off as he warned her to pray to her old gods; to prepare herself spiritually... but she realized with alarm that she didn't know how.

As if clinging to life itself, she kicked her horse and rode off.

She looked back, but he was nowhere to be seen.

By the time she returned to the ranch, Kaiulani was feeling very shaken. Her friends asked if there was anything wrong, as she looked so pale.

They put a blanket around her shoulders and she began to tell them of the incident.

Most of them told her not to worry, as it was typical of the old people in this region; to take the old Hawaiian ways so seriously, but Prince David Kawananakoa was very disturbed by the story, when it was related to him.

I n the middle of January, a group of revellers from the ranch, formed a riding party and headed off into the crisp cold air and soft green hills characteristic of Waimea. They were caught in a sudden downpour and drenched while they scrambled to don the raincoats attached to their saddles. The saturating rain of Waimea blows sideways like an icy knife that cuts and chills to the bone.

Kaiulani pulled her coiled hair loose, shook her head and went galloping off into the storm.

Her friends called out after her; to be sensible and cover up or she'd catch her *"death of cold"*.

But with a fatalism that had lately become part of her makeup. she replied: *"What does it matter? What have I got to live for?"*

Then off she went, swallowed up by the mist and driving rain, until her friends could no longer see her.

Probably Kaiulani's last letter to her father written from Mana on January 6, 1899:

Dearest Pa,

Many thanks for your letter. I am glad to know you have been enjoying yourself. You seem quite gay with your reception for the officers. I hope it will be successful - I hear the little men are rather nice. Tho'they don't speak much English.

Of course I don't mind lending Ainahau to any of our own friends. I only regret I won't be there to attend the reception. We are all well and it goes without saying we are enjoying ourselves immensely–

We had more then enough fun at the Ball in Waimea. All the people were in their best clothes, and had on their best manners. The Jarretts asked us to it, and they provided supper for our party, and very good it was too.. I did not dance very much as I was too amused watching the Country Bumpkins.

We left at 12 o'clock as there seemed to be an unlimited supply of liquor going around, and I knew the people would enjoy themselves better if we were not there. We went in the only conveyances there are to be had, between Hamakua and this side of the Island. Hardly any springs and the road was a thing to dream of - once I thought sure we would never right ourselves again.

It had been raining all that day (Friday) and Saturday we could not see twenty yards away - the fog was so thick. We left that evening for Mana in spite of the weather. My goodness the rain cut one's face like hail and it was blowing like cats and dogs. We got home at 7:30, wet to the skin, but thanks to a warm bath and warm drink and our dinner, we were none the worse for it.

The men were obliged to stay at the Hotel, and as luck would have it, the night of the dance, Capt. Lydig's luggage got taken to Puopetu. Sam Parker gave it to the man who drove us to the dance and told him to give to C.L. When we came back at midnight we found it still in the carriage. It seems they had all got soaked through out shooting, and instead of going to the dance, Capt. Lydig had to go to bed! I fancy he and Major Nicholson were very much disappointed at their accommodation, which I think was very ungrateful of them, when the girls were sleeping 8 in a room - they ought to consider - there were besides the family, Cupid and wife, David, Stella Cockett, Leihulu, Kitty and Mrs. Robt. Parker, Dorcas Richardson, Capt. Ross Sproull, Capt. L. Maynn, myself and Hilda and Mary, besides the family... there have been over twenty-eight ever since the wedding... you know about the size of the houses.

Tuesday we rode over to Waipio, got there about 3:30 p.m. there were quite a number of natives called and during the evening the natives came and serenaded us. As there was a good floor we had some dancing. We all turned in about midnight, but they kept it up till morning. The next morning we took a ride around the valley, unfortunately it began to rain, so I had no time to see my land or rather our land. I an sorry as I would have liked to have seen it.

We had to hurry as Lumaheihei was afraid of the Pali being too slippery. I never rode up such a place in all my life. I was simply hanging on by my teeth. We had a splendid ride home, jumping logs and pig holes–

A good many of the party go home today - I mean the native relations. Our plan is to leave for the volcano, taking the Kinau, then leaving for Kailua on the following Monday... We get to Hilo on Wednesday evening staying there until Friday at John Baker's place. Go up to the volcano on Friday or Saturday and leave on Sunday for Punahuu to catch Mauna Loa.

David goes down on the Kinau today to bring up the Dowager. Helen and Stella Cockett and Mr. Parker go up with me to volcano. Being a stockholder, Sam can get cheaper rooms there. Eva and Frank spent Xmas with us here.

I want you to send me my money for this month, what is left and also the $40 for January - I may not need it, But I want to have it any way. Please don't forget. (A belated Merry Xmas follows)

Merry Xmas to you all. My love to the family. I am so very sorry Helen has been so seedy. What was the matter with her? Tell Elsie to send up my holokus without fail. I want them badly. Send me up some Bromo Quinine pills, also get me headache powders No.75618 from Hollister - We never ordered sardines in November. One dozen bought for my party by Patty.

Our love to you all, and with much for yourself from,

> *Your Loving*
> *VIKE,*

Koa will tell you all news.

On January 24th, a Honolulu newspaper reported: *"Princess Kaiulani is quite ill at the Parker home at Mana, Hawaii. Governor Cleghorn leaves for Mana on the Kinau today."*

Cleghorn took the family physician, Dr. Walters, with him, to examine Kaiulani.

Anxious about their Princess' health, Honolulu readers soon learned from the newspapers that *"Princess Kaiulani is much improved. She and her father Gov. Cleghorn will return to Honolulu on the next sailing of the Kinau."*

Kaiulani was carried on a litter from the Parker Ranch to Kawaihae and onto the steamer *Mauna Loa,* as the *Kinau* had sailed without her.

By now, Dr. Walters had diagnosed her illness as *"inflammatory rheumatism"* with the complication of *"ex-opthalmic goiter."*

Kaiulani was in great pain throughout the rough sea journey back to Honolulu. Hawaiian crew members on the ship were very worried about the comfort of their precious passenger. They came by her cabin often with extra blankets, the few cushions or pillows on board; anything they had to offer. Back at Ainahau, her home in Waikiki, Kaiulani was put to bed in her darkened room. Her father sat for long hours beside her four-poster bed. Friends called daily to see her, the tracks of many carriage wheels furrowing the long dusty driveway between the phoenix palms.

By the beginning of March, Kaiulani's condition had not improved.

Doctor Walters, puzzled that Kaiulani had not responded to treatment, called in Doctor Miner to assist him and both doctors employed all their medical skills to arrest the rheumatism that was now dangerously attacking the patient's heart.

She had a bad turn on Saturday morning, March 5th, but throughout the day she seemed to show signs of improvement as the doctors continued to labor over her.

But just after midnight, the relentless illness began its work of prying her from life once again. Kaiulani tried to sit up. Her swollen throat had choked off her voice and she looked imploringly at Dr. Miner through half-closed eyes filled with pain.

The exhausted doctor patted her hand helplessly, and sent for the family to assemble in the sickroom.

Monday, March 6th, 1899 - from midnight to 1:30 a.m., Kaiulani's breathing was very unsteady. Dimly, through glazed eyes, she saw Koa, Helen Parker, Kate Vida, her half-sisters Helen and Rosie, and her father's stricken face leaning close beside the bed.

The clock had laboriously ticked to 2 a.m. when Kaiulani moved convulsively and cried out one muffled word. Some said she called *"Mama!"* Others thought it was *"Koa!"* or *"Papa!"*

Suddenly the room was very still.

Kaiulani was gone.

For many miles around, anxious people, awaiting news of the Princess, knew the precise hour of her death, because at 2:00 a.m. her pet peacocks began screaming wildly. Loud and long, their almost human cries pierced the night.

Drs. Miner and Walters gave the cause of death as cardiac rheumatism and ex-ophthalmic goiter. Their opinion was that she might have recovered from either ailment, but the combined assault was too much for one who was never constitutionally strong.

Kaiulani was twenty-three years and almost five months old at the time of her death.

All day Wednesday Kaiulani lay in state at Ainahau.

The newspapers were full of reports:

"The servants, many of whom had known Kaiulani since she was a baby, filed past her body, and gave way to uncontrollable grief. Scattered about her as she lay peacefully sleeping, were dozens of orchids and orange blossoms of purest white."

"Out in the grounds, mournful dirges of the band mingled with the wailing of the older natives as their voices rose now and then in the weird chanting of ancient meles."

"All day long the beautiful avenue leading to the residence at Ainahau, was crowded with people who came to pay their last respects. Throughout the spacious grounds, groups of Hawaiians were scattered, giving way to true spontaneous grief, as they clung together throughout the shrubbery, and under the banyan."

Among the small but loyal band of foreigners who defended the Monarchy was one Joseph O. Carter.

On the death of the Queen's niece he wrote the following letter:

Honolulu, HI
March 9th, 1899

Her Majesty
Liliuokalani,
Washington D.C.

Dear Madam, It is with the most profound sorrow that I convey to your notice of the death of your niece the Princess Kaiulani.

She passed away, after much suffering at two o'clock a.m. of the sixth instant.

In previous letters I told you of her serious illness, but until the first of the current month, I entertained hopes for her recovery. As soon as possible after hearing of her death, my wife Liliu and I went to Ainahau and met with the nearly heart-broken father and other relatives. As your representative, Mr. Cleghorn discussed with me plans for the funeral ceremonies. Mr. Dole offered

the Throne Room of the Palace for the lying in
state of the remains of the Princess.

Mr. Cleghorn decided at once that such a disposition of the remains was impossible in which
decision I supported him, but after much thought
the offer of a State funeral by the Executive was
accepted. Of course I should have preferred a sim-
pler funeral but one which would have been the
expression of more sincerity and sympathy. However, reasons were given why the State ceremony
should be permitted. Yesterday the remains lay at
Ainahau and thousands of people viewed them,
including all classes and conditions of our population.

On Saturday next, the remains will be in the
Kawaiahao Church in Casket and the public allowed to view them. The funeral will be on Sunday next at 2 p.m. Program of procession and
order of exercises not public yet.

I learn since this letter was commenced that
Prince David (Kawananakoa) has loyally and
generously assumed the charge of expenses incident to the funeral (on the authority of J.F.
Colburn) and if I had known of this in time I should
have urged a funeral on different lines, one that
Royalists could have directed.

Hawaiians are not altogether pleased to see
Mr. Dole's officers so prominent in the conduct
of affairs. Strangers in this city comment on the
wrong done to Hawaiians and their aliis by the
American Government taking Hawaii nei from the
hands of Mr. Dole and his government.

Accept from me and the members of my family sincerest sympathy in your bereavement.

Very truly yours
J.O. Carter.

The funeral observances were transferred to Kawaiahao Church. The casket of carved koa wood was borne into the church and placed on the bier in front of the platform. Covering the bier was a purple plush pall, lined with yellow silk, over which was spread the yellow feather pall of royalty.

A newsman wrote the following:

"Around the bier were arranged the large kahilis... Royal insignia... some twenty in number."

"Fragrant maile was wreathed around the pillars of the Church, while from the center of the Arch was suspended an emblematic white dove with outstretched wings."

"At the head and foot of the bier on stands were floral crowns... one of white carnations and the other of ilima and maile."

"High up on each side of the organ pipes were hung the Royal Standards of Kaiulani and Likelike."

"At all times both at Ainahau and the church, four Hawaiian kahili beaters or wavers stood on each side of the casket, silent and at periodic intervals of about 3 minutes, would slowly bend forward their kahilis to meet their opposites, and pausing awhile... or with one or two slow lateral motions would raise them again and bring them to shoulder."

"Hawaiian songs and chants were heard throughout the night."

153

"It rained all day Saturday, but Sunday morning, the day of the funeral, there was a glorious burst of sunshine... Scheduled for 2 o'clock, people began gathering at 10 a.m. There was a huge crowd mostly on foot, inside and outside the Church."

Bishop Willis of the Episcopal Church conducted the service, while the organist played *"In Memoriam"* written for Likelike's passing in 1887 and not played since.

One of Kaiulani's recent beaux, Andrew Adams sat for hours, heartbroken beside Kaiulani's casket. He had once given her a riding saddle which became her favorite. Cleghorn gave his permission for it to be in or near the casket when she was laid to rest.

As Kaiulani was laid beside her mother, Princess Likelike, in the Royal Mausoleum, the 23rd psalm was chanted by St. Andrews Priory girls.

Two *kahili* bearers preceded the procession out of the Church carrying two magnificent *kahilis* of fresh maile intertwined with ilima leis. They were the gift of Prince David Kawananakoa.

Twenty-seven *kahili* bearers surrounded the catafalque. As the casket was placed on it the old Hawaiians began wailing and chanting *meles*.

A large double rope of black and white attached to the catafalque, extended through the church grounds and out into the street. Two hundred and thirty Hawaiians who had coveted the honor, drew the body of the Princess with this rope, to her last resting place... the Royal Mausoleum in Nuuanu.

The newspapers reported: *"Amid tolling of bells, booming of guns, the funeral dirge played by the band; the wailing and chanting of the natives; the long*

*procession started on its way to the Royal Tomb...
through King St. to Alakea... Emma St. to Vineyard...
to Nuuanu... Over 20,000 people lined the streets.*

A few days after her death, a local paper wrote:

*The fortune of Kaiulani is not a large one. She
has been in receipt of an allowance from the Hawaiian Government, and quite recently the best men in
the country to a considerable number, petitioned Congress to continue an allowance to one deprived of
wealth and exalted position through no fault of her
own.*

In the weeks following Kaiulani's death, hundreds
of letters poured into Honolulu from all over the
United States, some offering sympathy to her grieving family, but a great number, addressed to members
of President Dole's reigning government, accused
them personally, often not in the most polite language,
of causing the Princess' untimely death.

One letter addressed to Sanford B. Dole, carefully written in copperplate style and accompanied
by another page bearing twenty-five handwritten signatures, was postmarked Atlanta, Georgia. For three
lengthy paragraphs it ramblingly scolded Dole and
his *"puppets"* for *"stealing the Princess' Royal inheritance'* and *"snatching away the Throne she was
prepared all her life to occupy"*. The letter closed by
assailing *"the cheap adventurers who invaded the
Hawaiian Islands just to make money"*.

The letter was signed:

"Princess K's Friends in the South."

After Princess Kaiulani's death in March, 1899,
the Advertiser wrote of her:

"Everyone admired her attitude. They could not do otherwise. Her dignity, her pathetic resignation, her silent sorrow appealed to all. The natives loved her for her quiet, steadfast sympathy with their woe, her uncomplaining endurance of her own. The whites admired her for her stately reserve, her queenly display of all necessary courtesy while holding herself aloof from undue intimacy. It was impossible not to love her..."

HO'OLOLI: *(To transform)*
And when Hawaiians die...
They change physical form according to their
*   kuleana... The claim of their family to the*
*   protection of a certain spirit.*
So look to the myriad forms of life in the Islands.
For the souls of departed Hawaiians are blowing
*   in the wind*
Or flowing in the lava from a volcano's core
Or dancing in the fire-lace flung from its red mouth
Or flying as the pueo, the mysterious owl
Or crackling across the sky as thunder and light-
*   ning*
Or slicing through blue ocean waters as sleek
*   sharks*
Or lying still in fire-lit streams by night...
Long and dark as the mo'o, the water-spirit with
*   gleaming eyes.*